A Mind of Your Own

*A good book is the precious life-blood
of a master spirit, embalmed and treasured up
on purpose to a life beyond.*

JOHN MILTON
1608–1674

By the same author

Mind to Mind
Mind Magic
Mind Waves
Mind Workbook
My Life as a Medium
The Infinite Mind
Clear Your Mind
Free Your Mind

A MIND OF YOUR OWN

A Book for Life

———◆———

BETTY SHINE

HarperCollins_Publishers_

HarperCollins*Publishers*
77–85 Fulham Palace Road,
Hammersmith, London W6 8JB
www.**fire**and**water**.com

Published by HarperCollins*Publishers* 1998
5   7   9   8   6

ISBN 0 00 653019 2

Printed in Great Britain by
Clays Ltd, St Ives plc

This book is dedicated to the memory
of my dear friend
MICHAEL BENTINE

From quiet homes and first beginning,
Out to the undiscovered ends,
There's nothing worth the wear of winning,
But laughter and the love of friends.

HILAIRE BELLOC
1870–1953

Introduction

❧

*Every quotation contributes something to the stability
or enlargement of the language.*

SAMUEL JOHNSON
1709–1784

THIS BOOK is an A–Z of experiences. Its aim is to help people with various aspects of their lives, to strengthen character and balance temperament. It can be dipped into again and again, whenever the appropriate help is needed. But the magic of this book will only be revealed when you have read every word.

Each word opens with a classic quotation to demonstrate that, although the world changes around us, human beings never change. We experience thoughts and emotions the same as people did centuries ago, and we still have the same problems. You may find that the quotation alone carries the age-old wisdom you seek.

Following a short insight from me, each key word also has a visualisation and an affirmation. The visualisation is short so that you can 'live' it as you read it. It is a trigger for the imagination and the self-healing process. See it in your mind, picture it from beginning to end, and you will find where the main problem lies. Then you can make the right decisions and change your life. If a particular visualisation does not in any way apply to your circumstances, you can modify it or create your own – that is why I have called the book *A Mind of Your Own*.

Many people believe that they cannot visualise, but if you ask them to remember a person or place that has been special to them, the pictures and feelings flow. Remember, the blockage is within *you*. Take your key and unlock the doors of your mind – you will be amazed at what you find.

Finally, you will find an affirmation at the end of each word to take with you when you close the book. It is the key to the rest of your life.

This is a book of life. In it you will find every emotion. You will laugh, you will cry, but you will never be bored. Enjoy!

Betty Shine

A MIND OF YOUR OWN

1

Abuse

*Whatever you do, stamp out abuses, and
love those who love you.*

VOLTAIRE
1694–1778

No ONE SHOULD have to tolerate abuse of any kind, and there can be no excuse for this abominable practice.

Mental or physical abuse to any living thing should never go unchallenged or unreported. Never condone this behaviour.

Visualisation: **You become aware that your best friend is continually abusing his girlfriend. When you confront him with it he excuses himself by explaining that, although he loves her, she irritates him. You try to reason with him, but to no avail. Are you going to stand by or give him an ultimatum?**

Either he treats his girlfriend with respect, or he loses your friendship. It's a tough decision but you follow through, because you know that you do not want to have these bad feelings in your life. Even a bystander *can* take action.

Affirmation: There is no excuse for abuse.

2

Accidents

*Now and then
there is a person born
who is so unlucky
that he runs into accidents
which started out to happen
to somebody else.*

DON MARQUIS
1878–1937

HAVING READ THE QUOTATION OPPOSITE you may find yourself thinking that you *are* that person. Think again. Through healing, I have found that the majority of accidents occur when people are under stress. If, as you read this, an accident has already taken place, then you are probably dealing with it at this moment. Your immediate reaction will also be that you do not want it to happen again, because the other problem you are having to deal with is shock.

My ability to see the energy system clairvoyantly has enabled me to study the tremors that occur within the body after an accident. You have probably experienced these tremors yourself, when you have dropped and smashed a piece of china and found that your hands are trembling as you pick up the pieces. What can you do about it?

Prevention is always better than cure. First of all, think before you act. A minute of your time could save a life. The pace of life is getting faster, and to counteract this you must steal a few moments before you act, so that you can have a little prime time for the rest of your life. Not only will you live longer, but the quality of your life will be greater.

Visualisation: You are running across a meadow of wild flowers – in SLOW MOTION. The slower you run, the more exhilarated you feel. Feel the fantastic lift as you put your life into perspective. Some things *can* wait.

When you avoid accidents, there is always another day.

Affirmation: A moment's thought could save a life.

3

Addiction

*In a consumer society there are
inevitably two kinds of slaves:
prisoners of addiction
and the prisoners of envy.*

IVAN ILLICH
1926–

WHENEVER ADDICTION IS MENTIONED, it is immediately assumed that the problem is drugs. Most of the time it is not. Nearly everyone, at some time in their lives, becomes addicted to something. It can be alcohol, tobacco, television, sports – one only has to think about football to realise how the power of addiction can take over your life. Chocaholics too certainly know all about addiction! Sugar is addictive in all its forms, and parents – with the best of intentions – start their children off on this road by giving them sweets for good behaviour or simply to keep them quiet. I have known people who have become addicted to vinegar, to the inhalation of substances like furniture polish, shoe polish, air fresheners and petrol. In fact you can become addicted to just about anything. This is the real danger. Most of the time you will be unaware that it is happening to you.

Obviously, there are real dangers in any kind of addiction. To overcome the ordinary everyday addictions, try using the following exercise twice a day.

Visualisation: **You walk into a small peaceful room, where you see a comfortable armchair; sitting in the chair, you become aware of a warm, comfortable glow as shafts of sunlight steal through the blinds.**

You have an overwhelming longing for your addiction. No matter what you do, this longing will not go away. You must now say three words: '*Please help me.*' You will immediately feel light and relaxed because you have, at last, realised that you have a problem. This is your first step to recovery.

For the first time you notice a table in front of you. On it is the cause of your addiction. Next to it is a small box, in the centre of which is a button. This is your life-line – when you feel desperate, you can press this button and it will switch off the addictive urge. You now have a choice. It doesn't matter which choice you make the first time. But if you make the wrong choice every time, then you need professional help.

It is amazing how the power of the mind can, eventually, help you to make the right choice. It will show you clearly how strong or weak you are, and then the guilt factor will take over. NEVER GIVE UP. YOU CAN DO IT.

Affirmation: Addiction is an affliction.

4

❦

Ageing

Youth, which is forgiven everything, forgives itself nothing:
age, which forgives itself anything, is forgiven nothing.

GEORGE BERNARD SHAW
1856–1950

PHYSICAL AGEING IS INEVITABLE and you cannot escape it, in spite of the beckoning fingers of advertising which promise everlasting youth. Beware!

There is a route that you can take to looking and feeling better, however, that costs nothing. By stimulating the energy counterpart of your physical body and strengthening your mind with visualisation, you can bring about a transformation. Your body will be the same, but it will glow with health. There will be a sparkle in your eyes as the power of your mind renews your enthusiasm for living. When this happens people do not see an ageing body, but are captured by the incredible essence that pervades everything around you. Friends will appear, as if by magic, because whatever it is that you have, they want it. I have seen very old, very beautiful people who know the secret. I am giving it to you.

Visualisation: **Every night, before you retire, sit on the side of the bed and close your eyes. You will see a blue door. Turn the key and open it. Walk through the door and gently close it behind you.**

You will immediately find yourself walking beside a shallow stream. Follow the stream until you see a fountain ahead of you. Standing beside the fountain, you watch as lacy cascades of water fill shallow bowls dotted around the outside ledge. Take one of the bowls and drink the contents. Gradually, you will feel the whole of your body and mind being rejuvenated. Aches and pains will disappear. Feeling light and lithe, you are able to move without restriction. You will feel weightless, as your mind – free of the burdens you have carried around for so long – revels in the freedom of movement, and you experience levitation of the spirit for the first time in your life. When you feel that it is time to return, open your eyes.

In time you will realise that you do not want to carry around the accumulated mental rubbish of a lifetime, and will discard it. Then you will know that it has been worth the effort.

Affirmation: I feel young. I am young.

5

❧

Aggression

As we jog on, either laugh with me, or at me,
or in short do anything, – only keep your temper.

LAURENCE STERNE
1713–1768

WHEN YOU ARE FACED with aggressive behaviour, back down and try to remain calm. It can be a very frightening experience. I have seen calm personalities explode and become aggressive when they have been pushed by unwarranted behaviour in others. Everyone has the capacity for becoming aggressive – it is there within us all, because we need to defend ourselves when physically attacked.

Self-discipline is the only way to keep this emotion under control, and the best way to do this is to explode on paper. As the thoughts come into your head, write them down, and keep writing until you are sick of the subject or personality you are attacking. Get it out of your system, because if you keep it there it will rear its ugly head at the most inopportune time.

If you happen to receive a letter written in anger, don't take it to heart. Allow the author a few weeks to calm down. Given time, they will probably regret having sent it.

Remember, we are only human, and we all have our failings. Forgive.

Visualisation: **You are sitting with a friend enjoying a relaxed conversation and a stranger nearby joins in the conversation. Annoyed at this intrusion you begin to feel aggressive. At this point visualise a plastic balloon inside your stomach, filling with air. Take a needle and prick the balloon before the hot air causes an explosion, injuring all those around you.**

Affirmation: Burst the bubble and stay out of trouble.

6

❧

Anger

Anger is a short madness.

HORACE
65–8 BC

L IKE A FIERY FLAME, anger begins in the pit of the stomach and within a few minutes pervades the whole of your body. It is only when you find yourself holding your head in pain that you realise what an impact it is making on your mind. It is at this point that you must make a decision. Are you going to let this unbelievable surge of adrenaline ruin your life and possibly that of everyone around you? Or are you going to allow discipline and logic to take over and channel your negative energies into something constructive?

You will not often have the amount of adrenaline that comes with anger at your disposal, so for starters, use it to get some of the lousy jobs that are part of your everyday life out of the way. If you have a car, wash and polish it instead of leaving it to someone else. If the house needs cleaning, get to it. Or walk the dogs that extra mile – they will love it and you will feel better. If you have no car, house or dogs, use your imagination and get rid of that first power surge somehow, for that is when really bad things can happen. Or you can try the following exercise.

Visualisation: Give yourself up to the moment. Picture a fiery red door. Open it. You find yourself in a large empty warehouse. Suddenly, the image changes and there is carnage all around you. You watch with horror as the debris silently slips into an abyss and you feel a force drawing you towards that abyss. This is decision time. Have you the strength and discipline to turn around and walk away? To return to sanity? If you have, you will find – perhaps for the first time – an inner peace which will support you throughout your life. If you cannot turn back, life will remain difficult until you find the strength to do so.

Affirmation: The anger will not consume me.

7

❦

Anxiety

When you're lying awake with a dismal headache, and
repose is taboo'd by anxiety,
I conceive you may use any language you choose to
indulge in, without impropriety.

W. S. GILBERT
1836–1911

FOR SOME PEOPLE, being in a state of permanent anxiety is the norm. Even when there is nothing specific to feel uneasy about, they imagine that something is missing from their lives. Having never experienced peace of mind, it becomes extremely difficult for them to dislodge such a long-standing habit.

Anxiety is a habit you cannot afford. It takes away the ability to see clearly and you make mistakes. However, minds that are fully occupied don't have the time to indulge in anxiety and are usually healthier for it.

Through healing, I have been able to cure this all too common habit, many times, only to see it return as soon as the voice of reassurance becomes unavailable. If you are serving a life sentence because of this problem, make time every day to practise the following exercise.

Visualisation: You find yourself walking down a corridor of closed doors. As you reach the doors they swing open. Anxious and fearful, you try to turn back, and then you hear a voice saying, 'Don't be afraid. I will walk with you.' You have a feeling of total peace and you walk on.

The first door swings open. You look inside – the room is empty. Leaving the door open, you move to the second door and open it, revealing a room full of sunlight. You open the third door and find a group of people meditating. The door to the fourth room reveals nothing more than three people in earnest conversation. But as the fifth door opens you come face to face with four miserable individuals. The negativity they radiate is so strong that you hurriedly close the door behind you. You know, without a shadow of doubt, that you do not want to join the unhappy people in the last room.

As you can see, most of the fears you had were unfounded. Those that weren't can be shut out of your life whenever they unnerve you.

There will be many doors in your life that will need to be investigated. But in the end the choice of leaving those particular doors open or closed will be yours.

Affirmation: Anxiety is counterproductive – I don't need it.

8

❧

Bitterness

Teach us delight in simple things,
And mirth that has no bitter springs;
Forgiveness free of evil done,
And love to all men 'neath the sun!

RUDYARD KIPLING
1865–1936

AT SOME TIME OR ANOTHER, everyone will feel the acidity of bitterness burning into their soul. It is a difficult emotion to deal with. When this happens, memories invade the privacy of your thoughts at all hours of the day and night, and the pain never seems to go away. It does not really matter whether the memories are true or false. They are there, and you have to get rid of them.

Try this exercise. Take a pen and paper and write everything down as it comes into your head, and continue to write until you feel hollow inside and completely washed out. When you have finished, DO NOT READ IT THROUGH – otherwise you will simply be feeding it back into your mind.

Find an old tin – deep biscuit tins are the best – place your notes in the tin and then put it into the sink where it will be safe. Put a match to the paper and watch it burn, knowing that as it does so your bitter thoughts will be reduced to ashes.

Keep repeating this exercise until you feel cleansed. Because at some time you just have to face the world again. It is called SURVIVAL.

Visualisation: **Sit down and close your eyes. You are in a garden and can hear the most beautiful music flowing through your mind, embracing your soul. You get up and start walking through the garden to find the source of the music, but it begins to fade. Then a voice says, 'When you are cleansed of all the bitterness, only then will you hear the full glory of the music.'**

Affirmation: Bitterness sears the soul.

9

❧

Blessings

Look to your health; and if you have it, praise God,
and value it next to a good conscience; for health is the
second blessing that we mortals are capable of; a blessing
that money cannot buy.

IZAAK WALTON
1593–1683

ALTHOUGH HEALTH IS OF PRIME IMPORTANCE in our lives, there are hundreds of small blessings that bring happiness into our everyday existence, and it is very comforting to remember these. Perhaps that is why you have turned to this page. But you may be reading this because you are having a bad day. If so, take a few minutes to run through the following visualisation.

Visualisation: **You begin to think about the small things that have made your life bearable. They might be recent or from many years ago. As each memory comes to life you will feel rejuvenated as the original pleasure that it gave you pulses through your being. Memories are real – they can never die.**

Affirmation: Life itself is a blessing.

10

❧

Books

True ease in writing comes from art, not chance,
As those move easiest who have learn'd to dance.
'Tis not enough no harshness gives offence,
The sound must seem an echo to the sense.

ALEXANDER POPE
1688–1744

MY LOVE AFFAIR WITH BOOKS began when I visited a public library for the first time. I must have been about three years old because I could only reach the books on the lower shelves. I clearly remember the dilemma caused by the fact that I could only borrow two books at a time. I wanted to take them all.

To achieve anything in this life we have to read books, whether it is for business or pleasure. The difficulty when buying a book is to make the right choice, especially when money is short. Even when you know what kind of book you want, a mistake can be costly, especially when there is a choice of authors in a particular field. That is why the following exercise is so useful.

Visualisation: **You are standing in a book store studying the titles and authors that are of interest to you. Running your hand over all the books, you suddenly remove one from the shelf and open it up. You may wonder why you have chosen that particular volume. It is because the soul of the author is in the energy of the book and will remain no matter how many times it is reprinted. Your hand, acting as a tool, has located a soul mate. Although you were unaware of it, you were practising psychometry, reaching out with your mind and connecting with psychic energy through touch.**

Always hold a book for some time before buying. Your instincts will do the rest.

Affirmation: Feel the vibes before buying.

11

Burdens

With aching hands and bleeding feet
We dig and heap, lay stone on stone;
We bear the burden and the heat
Of the long day, and wish 't were done.
Not till the hours of light return,
All we have built do we discern.

MATTHEW ARNOLD
1822–1888

B URDENS OF ANY KIND can cause havoc with your lifestyle, and particularly with your health. Although the mind and body can take an enormous amount of pressure, everyone has their breaking point. The art of dealing with any burden is to despatch it as quickly as possible.

Visualisation: You find yourself sitting on the top of a mountain. You are surrounded by many boxes. Looking up at the clear blue sky, you hear a voice calling your name. Then, a figure in white appears before you. 'Give me your burdens and I will deal with them,' he says. You gesture to the boxes, and the apparition smiles. 'I can see clearly now why you are so unhappy.' He claps his hands and the boxes disappear. 'They have now been dealt with,' he tells you. 'Walk tall, do not let burdens break your spirit. Let me carry them for you.' He touches your hand. 'Go! Live your life to the full. Surround yourself with friends and fill your life with laughter, for I will be with you always.'

Affirmation: I do not have to walk this path alone.

12

❦

Career

Weary with toil, I haste me to my bed,
The dear repose for limbs with travel tired;
But then begins a journey in my head
To work my mind, when body's work's expired.

WILLIAM SHAKESPEARE
1564–1616

TO BE SUCCESSFUL IN A CHOSEN CAREER is invigorating and exciting. Every day is a challenge. But no matter how successful you may be, it is always wise to be aware of the pitfalls. Be mindful of your health at all times, for without it your success will disappear overnight. Remember too that, whatever you give out will come back tenfold. Hold on to your integrity, for without it you are nothing. Good luck!

Visualisation: **You are in a room full of people. You see that those to the right face you with smiles and come forward to greet you. Look left, and the faces are bitter with hate and resentment. They cause you anguish. Make a promise to yourself that next time you enter the room there will be more people on the right than the left. Aim one day to be able to do this exercise one last time and find the left side of the room to be an empty space.**

Affirmation: Success is nothing without friends.

13

❧

Carefree

The learn'd is happy nature to explore,
The fool is happy that he knows no more.

ALEXANDER POPE
1688–1744

IT IS VERY DIFFICULT TO BE CAREFREE all the time. But you must find the time, on a regular basis, to indulge in this most exhilarating pastime. It is essential for your health. Once you have experienced the freedom and the sense of belonging to nature, I guarantee you will become hooked. Years of being worn down with pressure and responsibility will vanish. Your body will feel feather-light as you move around and your mind will become clear, enabling you to see – perhaps for the first time in your life – the real beauty of colour. If you find it difficult to become carefree, read on.

Visualisation: Finding yourself in the middle of a forest, you become increasingly uneasy as you find one path after another blocked by masses of tangled brambles. You are lost and cannot retrace your steps. Cold and weary, you sit down on the damp peat ground, first hugging your knees, then curling into the foetal position.

Then you hear a voice saying, 'Your body may be imprisoned by gravity, but your mind is not.' A white cloud dances around your head. 'You see,' the voice says, 'that is your mind, which can be released from the body with a single thought. Follow it.' Springing to your feet you follow the cloud, and as you do so the brambles disappear. It is only then that you realise that the brambles were an obstacle you had manifested yourself.

Affirmation: Everything is possible.

14

❧

Carers

Life may change, but it may fly not;
Hope may vanish, but can die not;
Truth be veiled, but still it burneth;
Love repulsed, – but it returneth!

PERCY BYSSHE SHELLEY
1792–1822

CARERS SEEM TO BE the least thought about section of society. Yet the job of caring is usually thrust upon individuals when they themselves are at their lowest ebb. Old age is one factor – if the patient is a partner or a member of the family, the carer is usually pressurised into believing that it is their duty to take on the burden of becoming nurse/housekeeper. When a fairly healthy person is put under this pressure, their own health will also suffer, no matter how much they may love the patient.

If you are a carer, please seek help from local societies and authorities. There may be someone who would be prepared to sit in for you occasionally. You might even be able to share the load a little more with other members of your family – don't be afraid to ask for support. You must have some space to yourself on a regular basis. Practising the visualisation exercise every day will help you.

If you are reading this and you are not a carer, but can find some time to spare – even if only a couple of hours a week – ask around your particular area and see if you can help.

Visualisation: Feel the sand between your toes as you walk along a deserted beach. Peace flows through your mind and body as the waves break along the shore, lulling you into a trance-like state. You feel light as the weight of responsibility is lifted with your spirits. This is your space – no one else can enter. Make good use of it.

Affirmation: I shall use my space every day.

15

❧

Caressing

Affection shown by a gentle touch,
Can still a troubled mind.

BETTY SHINE

THERE IS NOTHING quite like a gentle caress to soothe a troubled mind, especially when it is done with love. Babies thrive on touch, and throughout our lives we long for it.

The effect caressing has on the psyche can be clearly seen when one strokes an animal like a cat or a dog. The ecstasy they are experiencing is immediately apparent, and when it stops they beg for more. The majority of humans are not as demonstrative – if we were, life would be more pleasurable. The best way to overcome reticence and to enhance our lives is to practise the following exercise every day.

Visualisation: You are in a hospital. Walking around the wards, you are aware of the patients in their beds. They are sick but they are also sad, and in your heart you know the sadness is due to their loneliness. You walk towards a bed and stretch out your hand to the person in it. A look of gratitude, a sudden light in the eyes, is all the thanks you need. You feel good. Passing along the row of beds you give everyone a little of yourself, and when you leave there are smiling faces saying, 'Thank you.'

Now you remember how many times you had taken for granted a loving touch or caress given to you by parents, partner and friends when they wanted you to know how much they cared. You are overwhelmed by a feeling of guilt, and you long to touch these same people, to give back a little of what you had received. You make a promise to yourself that you will never take a caress for granted again.

Affirmation: It is more satisfying to give than receive.

16

❧

Chain letter

He gave the little wealth he had
To build a house for fools and mad;
And show'd, by one satiric touch,
No nation wanted it so much.

JONATHAN SWIFT
1667–1745

CHAIN LETTERS should always be destroyed. Someone is trying to control you, so the act should be immediate and final. Do not even consider reading them. The perpetrators hope to activate the guilt syndrome, and they can be extremely successful. I have seen the end results, and they can be tragic.

DO NOT READ — DESTROY.

Visualisation: **You receive a letter and, on opening it, realise that you are holding a chain letter in your hands. You begin to read it; gradually a feeling of guilt pervades your whole body. You ask yourself whether you have the right to destroy the chain as so many people have obviously taken part in its journey. There is another feeling within you, which is trying to surface — common sense. Will guilt prevail? No! Not wishing to be controlled by others, you see yourself tearing it into small pieces and throwing it away. Now you know you are free to choose your own path.**

Affirmation: I will strengthen my resolve not to be controlled.

17

❧

Character

What is character but the determination of incident?
What is incident but the illustration of character?

HENRY JAMES
1843–1916

WHEN, AS A CHILD, I was told to do something that was 'character building', I knew I would hate it. Those two words always filled me with dread. I also found it very odd that the two things I loved most, singing and reading, were *not* deemed character building but simply 'hobbies'.

Freezing walks in the rain, with the wind howling not just around me but through me, chilling my body to the bone, was supposed to be good for me, as was sport, which was agony.

Writing essays, however, was a doddle for me. Unfortunately, my English teacher did not like my style and said I did not fill the paper with enough detailed description. I was not, obviously, going to become a great literary writer, because endless descriptive passages bored me to tears (and, I have to admit, still do). Not one teacher had the sense to suggest that I might become a good journalist.

My first job as a messenger carrying printing plates to all the major newspapers and magazines in Fleet Street was the true beginning of my character building – long hours running up and down the stairs in every building, people shouting because the blocks were late, and returning to base in tears, thinking that I would rather be dead than carry on. But I had promised my mother that I would give a few shillings a week to the family income and had resolved not to let her down.

In the end it is your own spirituality that gives you the blueprint to build character. Those character building bricks are stacked up in your own psyche waiting to be released when you are strong enough to mix the cement to hold them together.

Visualisation: **You have promised a friend that you will always be there for them. One day you receive a call from them asking for help. Unfortunately, you are going through a difficult time yourself and do not feel able to carry out your original promise at this time. What are you going to do? Ignore the plea for help? Meet them and explain your own predicament? Or suggest that you give each other mutual support? Whatever you decide, do not forget that you need to be balanced spiritually and physically to maintain the whole.**

Affirmation: To build character I need balance.

18

❧

Charisma

*A quality which inspires great
enthusiasm and devotion
Needs to be disciplined
when dealing with emotions.*

BETTY SHINE

CHARISMATIC PEOPLE can enhance or destroy our lives. I have seen the effects of the latter at first hand. If parents are not careful and their child becomes aware of his or her own charisma at an early age, they will forgive their offspring everything and a control freak will come to the fore. However, I have also met people who, unaware of their charisma, fill others with such warmth that life seems infinitely more bearable in their presence.

When faced with a charismatic personality, study them and listen. Then you should have no problem deciding which of the two categories they fall into.

Visualisation: Taking a stroll one evening, you notice a stream of people entering a lecture hall. Intrigued, you join them. Having been informed of the subject matter of the lecture, you decide to stay, and you are immediately entranced by the charismatic nature of the speaker. Within minutes you feel the atmosphere in the room changing until it is charged with emotion bordering on hysteria. You are being told to believe, at all costs. Looking around, you see the faces of the audience contorted with fervour. You decide it is time to leave. A member of the audience follows you outside and asks you why you are leaving so early. 'I am leaving,' you tell him, 'because I like to choose the paths I tread, and I did not find peace in this place.'

While walking home you remember a teacher at school, who not only had masses of charisma but who regularly, and with humour, put himself down. And you realise that it had been an act so that his pupils would not think he was God and take everything he said as gospel. He captured their interest with his charismatic personality, made them listen, and then, when he thought they had understood, he made them laugh. He wanted them to enjoy his lectures but keep their own thoughts intact.

Affirmation: When I meet a person with charisma I will be cautious.

19

❧

Charity

By different methods different men excel;
But where is he who can do all things well?

CHARLES CHURCHILL
1731–1764

I F PEOPLE WERE MORE CHARITABLE to each other, the world would be a better place. Charity takes little effort and can give much pleasure. Remember, whatever you give out will come back to you when you are at your lowest ebb, so that it will have the maximum effect.

Visualisation: You are preparing for the first exhibition of your sculptures, and feeling very vulnerable. Will it be a success? Or will it be a great flop? An acquaintance asks for a preview of your work. After a while he walks toward the door. 'I have to go,' he says.

'Well, that was quick,' you reply. 'Before you leave, will you tell me what you think of my art?'

He grimaces. 'Not much, I'm afraid.' As he leaves, you feel as though someone has hit you in the stomach.

Later, that same evening you remember a similar criticism that you had levelled at a friend when he had needed encouragement, and make a promise to yourself that, in future, you will try to be more charitable towards others.

Affirmation: Charity toward others will enhance my own life.

20

❧

Chatting

You must lie upon the daisies and discourse in novel
phrases of your complicated state of mind,
The meaning doesn't matter if it's only idle chatter of
a transcendental kind.
And everyone will say, as you walk your mystic way,
'If this man expresses himself in terms too deep
for me.
Why, what a very singularly deep young man this
deep young man must be.'

W. S. GILBERT
1836–1911

I LOVE THE WAY Gilbert puts everyone in their place. This quotation is especially applicable to the psychic world. And what better relaxation could you find than having a chat with a friend? Hours pass as you let your hair down and bare your soul, cleansing and healing simultaneously. It will never go out of fashion and cannot be surpassed as food for the soul. Highly recommended.

Visualisation: **Arriving home after a miserable day at work, you sit down in your favourite chair and try to relax. But the adrenaline is still flowing, so you walk to and fro as you relive your day. Glancing at the telephone, you decide to ring a friend. After twenty minutes of idle chat, spiced with some cynical humour, you feel refreshed and ready to face the world again.**

Affirmation: Don't feel flat – have a chat.

21

Cheating

I to my perils
Of cheat and charmer
Came clad in armour
By stars benign.

A. E. HOUSMAN
1859–1936

CHEATING IS LOATHSOME and deprives the cheat of integrity. Stealing something you had no right to have can only bring misery. Only achieving your goals on your own merit will bring happiness and fulfilment and the knowledge that you can survive alone.

Visualisation: You have the opportunity, before sitting for an important examination, to scan the questions and answers. You take it, even though you know you have the ability to pass without cheating. Unfortunately, someone has seen you and you are promptly disqualified. Your action has spoiled your chances of a bright future, brought shame on your family, and humiliation on yourself. It simply was not worth it, was it?

Affirmation: My achievements will always be a product of my own unique ability.

22

Cheerfulness

I have tried too in my time to be a philosopher;
But, I don't know how, cheerfulness
was always breaking in.

OLIVER EDWARDS
1711–1791

IF YOU WERE BORN with a cheerful disposition, be thankful. Heaven alone knows how much the world needs the continued injections of this gift. At work or play, those that have it are a joy to be with and are much sought after for the light they bring into people's lives.

Misery is so much easier to come by. Don't let it put out *your* light.

Visualisation: Faces of misery are all around you. As you study them you realise how sad and comical they are. Vowing never to project this image of yourself, you smile, and the world begins to feel a brighter place. No matter what problems you are encountering at this time in your life, smile, and smile again. Resolve to have a cheerful disposition at all times, and to introduce others to your secret formula.

Affirmation: Spreading cheer will bring others near.

23

❧

Christmas

Heap on more wood! – the wind is chill;
But let it whistle as it will,
We'll keep our Christmas merry still.

SIR WALTER SCOTT
1771–1832

EVEN IF YOU ARE NOT RELIGIOUS, you should still perceive Christmas as a time for renewal, and take the opportunity to strengthen positive attitudes and add new ones. Looking back at the old year could give you some pointers as to how not to make the same mistakes again. Taking responsibility for your own life in this way means that you cannot continue to blame others for your mistakes, and you can now give yourself a pat on the back for the things you get right.

Those who are still aware of the spiritual meaning of Christmas are no doubt disturbed by the materialism that has come to shroud this special day. For some, Christmas has become a cause for financial stress, the effects of which continue throughout the following year. Expectations to buy bigger and better gifts can turn something joyous into a never-ending nightmare. Families should monitor this and step in with suggestions to relieve the burden. Make your own rules – above all, do not allow materialism to make this day of all days an occasion that your families dread.

Many people go on holiday to escape, but it is sad that many families will miss celebrating together, and friendships that could be renewed are forgotten. This is the one time in the year love should be at the top of your list.

Visualisation: **Old and alone, you sit by the fireside remembering Christmases of long ago. Money was sparse, so the paper chains were home-made, as were the decorations on the tree that stood by the window to cheer passers-by. The only presents were apples and oranges and a small chocolate in each sock, but they were always received gratefully.**

The turkey was the main attraction, and everyone would sit entranced as the first slices were cut and handed round. You would not see this again for another year. Later, carols were sung – everyone was happy and laughter rang through the house.

Thousands of children, both in this country and around the world, have never received a gift. So how about giving cheaper presents, and sending the remainder of what you would have spent to someone whose life may be saved by your generosity. It is no use just 'caring' – you have to *show* that you care. This way we can bring back the true meaning of Christmas.

Affirmation: I will keep the spirit of Christmas through the year.

24

❧

Clairaudience

Lives of great men all remind us
We can make our lives sublime,
And, departing, leave behind us
Footprints on the sands of time.

HENRY WADSWORTH LONGFELLOW
1807–1882

CLAIRAUDIENCE IS THE ABILITY to hear voices of people from other dimensions. From my own experience I have found it much easier to pass on messages to my sitters when receiving clairaudient communication, especially if the voice is loud and clear. That is an added bonus.

It is widely assumed that this gift is limited to mediums. This is not so. I have listened to many fascinating accounts of clairaudient messages that have been given to apparently non-psychic people. And it can happen at any time. It depends entirely on whether the mind energy has extended enough to link in with another dimension.

The best way to expand the mind energy is to meditate. If you find this difficult, then simply day-dream. You may not hear voices but your awareness will increase, and this in itself will enhance your life.

Visualisation: **Imagine a halo around your head. It is pure white, and the light is dazzling. It begins to expand outwards and upwards towards the universe. From out of space, shafts of light appear and touch the halo, as if to coax it ever closer to the spirit world. Stay in this space for as long as you wish, then watch as the halo returns to normal. This experience will stay with you forever.**

Affirmation: I will practise expanding my mind energy every day.

25

❧

Clairsentience

O Love, the interest itself in thoughtless Heaven,
Make simpler daily the beating of man's heart; within,
There in the ring where name and image meet.

W. H. AUDEN
1907–1973

CLAIRSENTIENCE IS THE ABILITY to decode imagery that comes from other dimensions as it appears like ticker-tape across the mind. The experience is rather like seeing the words of a poem in your head. If you close your eyes and think of a familiar poem, you will know what I mean. Unfortunately, the majority of the messages race across the mind so quickly that it is sometimes difficult to make sense of them.

For non-psychics, the closest comparison would be intuition.

Visualisation: **This exercise is for psychics and non-psychics alike. With your eyes closed, think of a favourite poem, quotation or affirmation. Observe the words crossing your mind. If they pass too quickly, actively slow them down. Remember that the mind is the control tower and your thoughts govern its operation. Practise every day – at the very least, it will help you to discipline your mind and your life.**

Affirmation: I am in control. I have the power to slow down.

26
❦

Clairvoyance

A Christian is a man who feels
Repentance on a Sunday
For what he did on Saturday
And is going to do on Monday.

THOMAS RUSSELL YBARRA
b.1880

CLAIRVOYANCE IS THE ABILITY to see clearly into the future. A talented clairvoyant can warn of dangers if it is obvious that you are taking a wrong path. In my experience, though, people only want to hear about the positive things. To reach a happy conclusion in a sequence of events, it is sometimes necessary to change your life and habits. This can be difficult, which is why the majority choose to forget the advice and carry on as usual. Some of my clients have walked very rocky roads after ignoring my guidance. This was not necessarily entirely negative though, because it taught them a lot about their own personality problems.

Your own intuition is the finest clairvoyance you can have. Have faith in your own instincts and you will be amazed at how right you can be.

I chose the quotation opposite with tongue in cheek, because for most people seeking clairvoyance, that is exactly how it is. And they are not all Christians!

Visualisation: **You find yourself walking rapidly through a dark tunnel. There is an urgency in your step because you know that when you reach the end of the tunnel your future will be revealed. The tunnel seems endless. Then, when you have almost given up, a glimmer of light appears in the distance. After a few more seconds you are standing in bright sunlight. Looking around, all you can see is a bleak landscape – no trees, bushes, streams, mountains, or wildlife. No life. Disappointed, you fall to the ground and cover your eyes. A sudden movement interrupts your thought. Lying beside you on the bare ground you notice a large box. Opening it, you find that it is filled with the most wonderful artists' tools and an incredible selection of paints and canvases. Then you hear a voice say, 'Did you really expect me to paint the landscape as well? What a boring life you would have if I had shown you the finished canvas.'**

Affirmation: I will paint a beautiful picture of my life.

27

Class

Bow, bow, ye lower middle classes!
Bow, bow, ye tradesmen, bow, ye masses.

W. S. GILBERT
1836–1911

UNFORTUNATELY, a class system exists in nearly every country in the world. But as individuals it should not present a problem, unless of course your work is affected by it. Class, as I can see it, should be about dignity, no matter what race or creed. We can all attain it. To be dignified is not to be blind, it is knowing how to project your image in the correct manner and keep your self-respect. It is not easy, when all around are seizing every opportunity to foul up your life – but it can be done. Try the following exercise.

Visualisation: **You are at a party where the guests are luxuriously dressed. You walk through the room, head high and feeling like a million dollars even though you are wearing a cheap outfit. People stare and gossip, making snide remarks as you pass. But as you look closer you realise they are unhappy and you feel sorry for them. There are a few who congratulate you on your outfit and immediately make you feel welcome. They have class. You turn around and smile kindly at the gossips. You have class too. But you also have the knowledge that you achieved everything you have with your own talent and integrity. That makes you special, and you feel good. Class is of your own making.**

Affirmation: I am a class act – and hard to follow.

28

Colour

The naked earth is warm with Spring,
And with green grass and bursting trees
Leans to the sun's kiss glorying,
And quivers in the sunny breeze;

And life is colour and warmth and light
And a striving evermore for these;
And he is dead, who will not fight;
And who dies fighting has increase.

The fighting man shall from the sun
Take warmth, and life from the glowing earth.

JULIAN GRENFELL
1888–1915

M Y HEALING ROOM was always filled with colour – cosmic colour. My patients saw the miracle for themselves as the room changed from sunflower yellow to pink, orange, blue, purple, and brilliant white. Very often these blended into a dense, vibrating rainbow of energy. And when it finally disappeared we knew that life without colour was no life at all.

I spent many years teaching my patients to use colour healing on themselves (which is well documented in my book *Mind Magic*). Even if you just add a bit more colour to your outfit by adding a bright scarf or tie, you will be giving yourself a more joyous and healthy existence.

When you go out, look around you and wonder at the changing colours of the seasons. Do you really notice them, or do you walk around blind to the beauty that surrounds you? And add colour to your home so that when you enter it you feel the atmosphere, warm and welcoming, wrapping itself around you.

Visualisation: You are standing in a room which has been decorated in dark colours. Nothing glows with life except the faint shafts of sunlight through the window. The half-drawn curtains are unmanageable and heavy and you are unable to let in more light. You feel claustrophobic and want to leave, but the door locked itself behind you when you entered the room. For a few moments you feel imprisoned and overwhelmed by this miserable colourless room, and you long to see the green grass and the daffodils that you had noticed on entering the property. With that single thought you are suddenly bathed in a daffodil yellow glow and you realise, for the first time, that if you colour your thoughts you will also colour your life.

Affirmation: The colours of my life must glow with an iridescent beauty.

29

❦

Comedy

This world is a comedy to those that think,
a tragedy to those that feel.

HORACE WALPOLE, FOURTH EARL OF ORFORD
1717–1797

IN THE DIM LIGHTS OF THEATRES, I have been able to observe the mind energies of the audience. When laughter fills the auditorium, the mind expands, giving the impression of balls of light dancing around. Having discovered and studied mind energy for so many years, I know that the energy blockages which cause stress throughout the body are being released, and the body is going into self-healing mode. One has only to look at that same audience when they leave the theatre to see that all around are smiling faces, lightness of step and an aura of well-being.

If you have the ability to make people laugh, use it. It is the finest healing of all. In the home it is a talent that can prevent arguments reaching a dangerous level. At the office it can work for you if you silently perceive the funny side of difficult situations.

Those of you who are not natural comedians should try the following exercise.

Visualisation: **Try to bring out the clown in yourself. Think of all the ridiculous situations that you could find yourself in and act them out in your mind. Then laugh at yourself.**

If you are a serious person, put yourself into a position mentally that resembles farce. Somewhere inside there is a comedian aching to get out.

Affirmation: Laugh every day and keep misery at bay.

30

⁂

Communication

*To do good and to communicate
forget not.*

THE BIBLE, HEBREWS

THE ABILITY TO COMMUNICATE is society's life-support system. Without it, we are lost.

Modern technology enables us to link with people around the world, and to access information in a few moments. Unfortunately, it can easily become a substitute for communication on a one-to-one basis. There is no substitute for the real thing.

The voice itself is magic, and can change the meaning of a single word by the way it is expressed. This, with the added vibration of the spoken word, can make one laugh or cry. There is no substitute when it involves the emotions – sympathetic words of comfort, words of wisdom and expressions of love. This is, and always will be, the finest way to communicate. However, technology is ideal for those who are by nature reserved, and is better than no communication at all.

If you do have problems in this area, speaking direct to people, see if the following exercise helps.

Visualisation: You are sitting at your desk deep in thought when the sound of the fax machine attracts your attention. Looking at the paper gliding through the machine, it becomes apparent that someone is very angry indeed. Reading through the printed page, you realise that a friend has misinterpreted a previous message. Unhappy about the situation, you send a new fax. Disturbed, you try to return to your work but you are unable to concentrate. The fax spills out a reply. It says, 'This matter was too important to be sent by fax. Still angry.'

Your working day in ruins, you pick up the phone and speak to your friend direct. When the conversation comes to an end, he says, 'I'm sorry to have misunderstood you. But your choice of words in the fax was inappropriate.' In fact, you had not changed the words at all. What had changed was the inflection and tone of your voice accompanying the words.

Although there has to be a place in the modern world for machines, especially in business, do not make a habit of replacing them totally in favour of that very special piece of communication equipment – the voice.

Affirmation: The art of communication is a gift. I must use it.

31

❦

Complaining

*Complain if you must
but only if it's just.*

Betty Shine

IN BUSINESS, people have come to expect complaints. Only time will tell whether or not they are justified. But people who complain continually make our lives a misery.

Through healing, I have found that unhappiness is often at the root of the problem. Cure that, and the complaints will cease. Very rarely do happy people complain, and when they do it is usually for a very good reason. There are those of course who never complain, for fear of reprisal or humiliation. If they make a complaint, then you can be pretty sure it is fully justified – listen to them, and learn from it.

Before airing a complaint yourself, think: Is it really that important? Are you being selfish? Are you looking for sympathy? Are you in need of attention? The list of possibilities is endless, but keep asking yourself questions. If you then still feel the need to complain, then go ahead. At least you will have reassured yourself that you are not complaining for the sake of it.

Visualisation: **You are sitting at work when the office moaner arrives. Not only do they disrupt your day, but it takes all of your strength not to be rude. When they leave you feel like a washed-out rag. On they go, from one person to another. Some suggest, kindly, that if their life is that bad then action should be taken. The advice is ignored.**

Another day at the office the same thing happens, only this time the complainant reckons that someone tried to attack them on the way to work. No one wants to listen. Later, that same person is found slumped over their desk. You notice they are covered in bruises. Everyone feels guilty – in this instance the complaint had been justified. But having listened to so many unwarranted complaints, how could you have known the seriousness of it this time?

Monitor yourself so that when *you* make a complaint, people will listen, and teach others by your example.

Affirmation: I will complain only when it is justified.

32

❧

Conceit

*Words are the tokens current and accepted for conceits,
as moneys are for values.*

**FRANCIS BACON
1561–1626**

CONCEIT IS AN EXTREMELY UNPLEASANT TRAIT. Arrogance of any kind is undesirable but self-love is repugnant in the extreme. It is totally different from loving and being comfortable with oneself. Conceit stems from such a lack of knowledge about oneself that the personality is tricked into thinking it is in some way exalted. Even worse, the individual also expects others to accept this image and to worship it.

I have met so many conceited people throughout my life that recognition of this condition is instant, and it takes only seconds for me to put distance between us. That might sound a little odd, but there are times when I have to share the same space at a function so the farther away I can stand from them, the better.

In many ways the condition is quite sad because these arrogant people crave recognition, and to encourage it they become poseurs. But the truth is that most of the time people avoid them like the plague. If you recognise yourself in this, read on.

Visualisation: **You are standing in a room full of people. You are dressed more garishly than anyone else, and you are longing to be noticed. But the conversational groups are not opening up to let you in. In fact, they are ignoring you. You feel sad, angry and alone, not having received the recognition that you believe you deserve. A waiter offers you a drink.**

'Am I not the most interesting and talented person around?' you ask him. 'Why am I ignored?'

'Talented you may be,' he replies. 'But not interesting, because you show no interest in others. You see, it is a two-way exchange. You do not play the game.'

Remember that the garishness and sadness that you have felt is the state of your mind. Do try to change. There is so much happiness around – seek it out and stop being conceited.

Affirmation: I want my life to be complete. I must rid myself of this conceit.

33
❧

Concentration

*Depend upon it, Sir, when a man knows he is to
be hanged in a fortnight, it concentrates his mind wonderfully.*

SAMUEL JOHNSON
1709–1784

Fᴿᴏᴍ ɪɴꜰᴀɴᴛꜱ ᴛᴏ ᴀᴅᴜʟᴛꜱ, lack of concentration is often caused by boredom. On the other hand, we are totally focused when we are enthusiastic about something. Talented teachers, though, can catch the imagination of their pupils, and induce concentration in even the most reluctant individual.

Enthusiasm for life is the trigger for stimulating poor concentration. When a special person enters your life and is able to make something happen for you, take the gift and enhance it with your own special talents. Finally, when you are able to walk alone, pass it on.

Visualisation: Whilst walking along a cliff path and looking out to sea, you become aware of a slight figure ahead of you dressed in a gold cloak. As you approach him, he turns and smiles. 'You do not recognise me?' he asks.

'No,' you reply.

The stranger looks into your eyes. 'I am your spiritual mentor. I have known you all your life.' Turning away, he waves his arms towards the sea. 'What do you see out there?'

Bored, but not wishing to be discourteous, you remark, 'Nothing much, just a few small boats.'

The stranger is intrigued. 'Don't you ever wonder what lies beneath the sea? Come. I want to show you.'

In a trance-like state you are transported into a world that you have never seen before. Walking along the sea bed, you are delighted by the colour and magnitude of this other world. You have seen pictures of deep-sea diving, but the reality is something quite different. To be able to touch the fish, the rocks, and swirling fronds of seaweed, and enjoy the varying colours in this magical landscape gives your life an added dimension. The stranger, pleased with your response, takes you further into the caves, uncovering secrets that only he could reveal. 'Now we will return,' he says, adding, 'If you want your life to have a magical quality, always look beneath the surface.'

Affirmation: Stimulation aids concentration.

34

❧

Confession

Confession is good for the soul?
No! Not always.

BETTY SHINE

BEFORE CONFESSING YOUR SINS to anyone other than your priest, THINK, THINK and THINK again about the misery you may cause. Small misdemeanours are quite easy to handle, and we are usually forgiven. It is the big sins that create havoc. Are you going to bare your soul to the victim simply to give yourself peace of mind, or because you are in a holier-than-thou mood? There are times when confessing becomes inevitable but there are also times when it is wise to maintain a dignified silence. Only you can decide, but imagine the scene and follow it through to the consequences. Where the emotions are concerned and hearts are broken, they very rarely mend without a scar. Please be very careful.

Visualisation: Go through the whole confession and consequences of your actions. Imagine every detail and think it through first. If you still wish to confess then do so, but be big enough to handle it in as dignified a manner as possible. If, on the other hand, you know that it could wreck someone's life, then delay the confession or discuss it first with a counsellor or your priest. Never confess on the spur of the moment.

Affirmation: I must think through the consequences before I make a move.

35

❧

Conscience

Labour to keep alive in your breast that
little spark of celestial fire, called conscience.

GEORGE WASHINGTON
1732–1799

IT IS OUR SPIRITUALITY or higher mind that dictates how we behave. I have known many people who have had no conscience at all, and who have destroyed everything and everyone in their path while still believing that they were spiritual. Conversely, I have known others who have had so much conscience that they imprisoned themselves with guilt, making their lives a complete misery.

Common sense combined with a healthy conscience is a good balance, resulting in a state, if achieved, that enhances not only our lives but the lives of others.

Visualisation: **You are being shown around a grand house when your host is called away. Left alone with a display of small but valuable trinkets, you have a sudden urge to own one of these pieces. You have never stolen before, but decide that as your host is very rich he will not miss it. Whilst you are turning a particularly beautiful piece in your hand, the lady of the house arrives. Introducing herself, she says, 'I see that you have fine taste. These pieces were given to me by my great-grandmother and are very special to us. They were given to her for her valour during the First World War. She saved many lives working as a nurse on the front line.' You feel mortified and, making your excuses, leave.**

Temptation is never very far away. But is it really worth giving into it, when you'll have it on your conscience for the rest of your life?

Those of you who have no conscience must become aware at some time that something very special is missing from your life. There is no amount of money or possessions that can buy you peace of mind, and without it, you will never be happy or healthy, for sooner or later you will have to pay the price. Looking on the positive side, there is always time to change. It is never too late.

Affirmation: I must heed my conscience at all times.

36

❧

Conversation

*Tomorrow a stranger will say with masterly good
sense precisely what we have thought and felt all the
time, and we shall be forced to take with shame our
own opinion from another.*

RALPH WALDO EMERSON
1803–1882

I LOVE THIS QUOTATION because it describes exactly that feeling of frustration you get when someone voices the thoughts you have had but have never expressed. It's made worse if they then receive compliments on their perception.

Everyone has interesting thoughts but there are people who are shy and cannot open up a conversation, fearful that they might look or sound stupid. Don't worry! If you have never been made to feel stupid then there is something radically wrong, because it shows a very sombre, staid and boring personality.

The art of good conversation is to open your mouth and talk. It really doesn't matter what subject you begin with, just get in there and become part of the action. If someone has a pretty brooch on their dress, compliment them on their choice. If it is a man, admire his tie – even if you don't like it, he does. Make him feel good about it. Compliments are great for bringing the feel-good factor into any gathering.

You may have a particular interest of your own, so talk about it. Give your companions some idea of what your daily life is like. You do not have to be ultra-intelligent, young, slim or glamorous to be entertaining. And smile! People are always attracted to others who bring some sunshine into their ordinary lives. When you are with other people always put some input into the conversation, otherwise it is left to one or two to carry the whole. Also you will not feel a drag.

Visualisation: **You have spent the whole evening choosing the right clothes and accessories. When you arrive at your destination and begin to mix, you are aware that some guests are standing about looking bored and others are in earnest conversation. Walk up to the bored individuals, say hello and tell them how happy you feel to have been invited (even if you're lying – a white lie now and then can be forgiven if it's in a good cause). Talk to them. Bring some life into their lives. Your hosts will be forever grateful. There is nothing worse than a gathering in which some guests talk non-stop and others won't talk at all. And while you are doing your bit, you'll probably enjoy it.**

Affirmation: Smile, speak, listen.

37

❧

Criticism

*I do not resent criticism, even when, for
the sake of emphasis, it parts for the time with reality.*

WINSTON CHURCHILL
1874–1965

CONSTRUCTIVE CRITICISM can plant a seed that, when nurtured, can bring about a transformation in our chosen career or hobbies. But negative criticism creates an aura of bitterness and resentment that can linger with us for ever. This is unforgivable, and can lead only to unhappiness and despair.

I have seen mediocre performances in the theatre blossom when sympathetic criticism had been given. The fact that someone cared had lifted the spirit and fired the imagination.

Visualisation: Having joined an advanced art class, you have just finished a picture and are sitting back trying to judge it objectively. Along comes the teacher, who takes one look and tells you that, in his opinion, it is a mess. He suggests that you tear it up and start again with a clean canvas. Totally humiliated, you try to do as he asks, but the hurt is deep and your mind is clouded. You are now incapable of the most simple task. You leave – with your painting.

You join a new art class. When the teacher looks at the painting, he tells you that he is most impressed with the unique way in which you use your imagination. He suggests that perhaps with a little discipline it could be so much better. You are inspired by his words and, after studying the picture, can see how creative his suggestions could be. As the images flow through your mind your brush works at the canvas and you know that something wonderful is going to happen. What a change those few words have made – so different from the first negative experience.

In this exercise, the reason for taking the picture away from the first class is to show that someone might eventually see your creation as a work of art. In this life, everything is so subjective.

You can change this exercise to suit your own career or hobby. The imagination has no boundaries and is the life-blood for the genius.

Whilst you were visualising, you could probably feel the pain and the joy caused by the contrasting criticisms. Remember that feeling when you are about to criticise others.

Affirmation: I am open to constructive criticism, but closed to negativity.

38

Crying

When we are born we cry that we are come
To this great stage of fools.

WILLIAM SHAKESPEARE
1564–1616

CRYING IS THE MOST therapeutic thing that you can do. That is, unless you allow it to go on too long, when it will result in headaches, swollen sinuses, red nose and an unattractive appearance. If the cause of your despair is tragic, then continue to cleanse your soul, for that is what crying is – a cleansing of the soul.

Scientists have found that tears contain a harmful chemical which can lead to a build up of toxins in the body, so releasing them can cleanse the body too. Crying is a healing process.

Visualisation: It has been a hot summer. Everywhere you look dust has settled on the trees, bushes and flowers, their dusty leaves limp and lifeless. Roads are covered in dirt which is thrown up into the air by every passing car. The air is polluted.

In the distance you hear the crash of thunder, and lightning flashes across the sky, and as big drops of rain begin to fall you glance out of the window. The landscape is being transformed. Trees are glistening with raindrops, bushes have an iridescent glow and the colours of the flowers are being restored to their natural glory.

As you cry, imagine this cleansing taking place within your body and mind. Get rid of the chemicals and glow within.

Affirmation: Cry – cleanse – heal.

39

❦

Cults

*Don't let us make imaginary evils, when you know we
have so many real ones to encounter.*

OLIVER GOLDSMITH
1730–1774

THE TYPE OF PERSON who runs a cult is one who is addicted to controlling others. Such people come in many guises, so beware. It is so easy, especially if you are lonely, to be attracted to a person or group of people who, on the surface, appear to be kind and helpful. But if there is any indication of any sinister aspects to their personality – get out. It is much better to be safe than sorry. Never make excuses for them, but remember, they want to control you and will seduce you with attractive promises.

Those who also practise black magic tend to have very short unhappy lives and unpleasant deaths, because they are attracting negative energies all the time, which they cannot escape and which will eventually destroy them. Remember, energy attracts like to like, so avoid the dark path at all costs.

Visualisation: You find yourself in a meadow. Looking up at the sky you can see low black clouds rolling towards you, threatening to engulf you. With one hand, make the sign of the cross in the air. The wind changes and the black clouds recede and a brilliant shaft of sunlight lights up your whole being. YOU HAVE CHOSEN WELL.

Affirmation: I will always look for the light in my life.

40

❧

Danger

Danger, the spur of all great minds.

GEORGE CHAPMAN
*c.*1559–1634

CHILDREN LOVE DANGER. Most of them court it because it is exciting. Out of sight of their parents they do all the dangerous things that adults have warned them not to do. Some children never grow up and as adults still seek out the danger in life. If the results are positive and eventually turn them into responsible human beings with a touch of the child within, then it is fine. But so many are irresponsible and leave others to pick up the pieces. If you fall into the latter category, read on.

Visualisation: You are sitting in the middle of a field, enjoying a family picnic when you decide to climb an old oak tree. The family urge you not to do it. The children say you are too old, which spurs you on even more. Your wife says nothing. But for one split second, as you look at her, you see for the first time the misery behind the façade, and you know that you have been the cause of all the unhappiness. You climb down and sit beside her, and say, 'I have just realised that I don't have to prove anything.' Her eyes look questioningly at you. 'Because,' you reply, 'you have achieved more in your life than I have with my stupid escapades.' She begins to cry. You make her a promise that from that moment on you will think only of her and try to erase the bad memories.

Affirmation: I must be responsible for my own actions and think of others whilst so doing.

41

✃

Death

Tell me, my soul, can this be death?

ALEXANDER POPE
1688–1744

I HAVE CHOSEN this quotation because during my work as a medium the voices of 'dead' people have told me that they also asked the same question when they realised that their mind had survived the physical death. They found the dimension in which they were now living so unbelievable – beautiful, peaceful and all-forgiving – until they were taught that Mind is everlasting and that love exists in a form barely known to us on Earth. The simple fact is that we cannot die. Our mind energy is attached to the physical body and brain until the body dies, then it leaves. But it does not disappear. It simply goes elsewhere.

We are not judged by others, but when we are shown our whole lives as if on ticker-tape, we judge ourselves, and choose a path to take us on to the next step of our universal journey.

Not only have I listened for years to survival messages and evidence from those who have left, and from those who have had near-death experiences, but my own meditation has taken me into realms of tranquillity and love that are beyond our comprehension in this world.

Living our lives to the full and giving love and compassion to others will enhance what we have now. It will certainly give more happiness and make more sense of life than always taking, always looking for a free ride. Remember, that you will have to atone one day.

Visualisation: **You have practised the art of meditation every day of your adult life. Although it is relaxing, your mind has never expanded to touch other dimensions and give you the joy that so many claim is there for the asking. One day, during meditation, you ask why? A few minutes elapse, and then you are shown images of yourself in different situations. In every one you are asking for something, never giving. That is your answer.**

Affirmation: I cannot die. My mind is everlasting.

42

❧

Destiny

Sow an act, and you reap a habit.
Sow a habit and you reap a character.
Sow a character, and you reap a destiny.

CHARLES READE
1814–1884

I BELIEVE IN DESTINY. Throughout your life you will dance from path to path, sampling the delights and the miseries and forming a character. You are destined to be whatever you become and, through becoming, you will arrive at your destination. Think carefully every step of the way, because your destiny is in your hands.

Visualisation: Form a picture in your mind of how you would like to appear to others at the end of your life. Then picture yourself surrounded by friends. Happiness abounds because you have given so much to each other.

A video appears and you all watch, joking and laughing at all the stupid things you have done throughout your lives. Then someone says, 'Well, at least we kept our sense of humour. Without that, everything we did would have been worthless.'

Think about it!

Affirmation: My destiny will be of my own making.

43

Destructiveness

Man, false man, smiling, destructive man.

NATHANIEL LEE
*c.*1653–1692

ONE ONLY HAS TO STUDY history to see the destructive nature of man. If you take the destructiveness of every human being and gather it together in armies, then it is not hard to imagine the outcome.

Then there is the self-destructive mode that is in all of us. Why is it that we often seem to destroy the things we love the most? I have looked for an answer and my conclusion is that there is not one answer but hundreds and that it depends on the unique personality of every one of us.

I am leaving you, the reader, to analyse your own thoughts and actions, for within you lies the answer to your particular problems.

Visualisation: **Before you destroy anything in your life, whether it is a friendship, loving relationship, the atmosphere at home, at work or any kind of physical destruction, examine your motives. Leap forward and visualise the outcome, and ask yourself whether you have done enough to save the situation or whether you have allowed the destructiveness in your nature to eliminate logic and common sense. If you still want to go ahead, then you must take responsibility for your actions.**

Affirmation: Something that has been destroyed can never be reclaimed.

44

❧

Detachment

And this the burthen of his song,
For ever us'd to be,
I care for nobody, not I,
If no one cares for me.

ISAAC BICKERSTAFFE
c.1735–1812

DETACHING ONESELF from a situation may seem difficult, but it is sometimes necessary to do this in order to avoid confrontation. However, to detach oneself when someone else is in need can be callous and inhumane. If you wish to do this then you must remove yourself from the situation altogether, to lessen the hurt that would be felt by others because of your actions.

At some time or another, everyone will find themselves on the receiving end of this kind of treatment. Unfortunately life is like that! There is no preparation, but knowing that it can happen will lessen the impact it has if it happens to you. But be mindful, the person who detaches themselves from somebody in need will find that they have destroyed a trust that can never be reclaimed.

Visualisation: **You have been asked to support a close friend who is in need. Knowing that it will interfere with your own life, you think about it before making a decision. Then a small voice in your head asks you to reverse the situation. It could be you in trouble. How would you feel if your friend detached themselves from *you* on this issue? The emotions welling up inside you are the same feelings that your friend is having at this moment. You know what your answer will be.**

Detachment of any kind has to be well thought out. It could isolate you later on.

Affirmation: I will always mentally reverse the situation before I make any decisions on detachment.

45

❦

Determination

Our deeds determine us, as much as we determine our deeds.

GEORGE ELIOT
1819–1880

DETERMINATION IS A SINGLE-MINDEDNESS that produces results. It is the backbone of the 'will to win at all costs' mindset, but if it is taken to extremes it can isolate the individual. Just how much determination we need for any specific task is open to question – a question that needs considerable thought. Never forget that we all have to interact with one another to achieve lasting results. 'Moderation in all things' are wise words in this instance.

Visualisation: You are determined to succeed, and so when you are offered the opportunity to realise your ambition you accept without hesitation. Within weeks you find that you have sold your soul. The contract is for two years, but during that time your determination helps you to survive.

Think about these two issues. On the one hand your determination, without thought, landed you in trouble. On the other it enabled you to survive. And when you have thought about them, remember them. Temper your impulse for determination with a dash of common sense.

Affirmation: I will always balance determination with realisation.

46

❦

Devil

The Devil watches all opportunities.

William Congreve
1670–1729

MANY PEOPLE SEE the devil as a real person. In fact, this particular entity is within all of us. It is a facet of our mind energy, a blueprint we have drawn with the imagination, and it is a facet which can destroy the host. Love is the only energy that can eliminate the thought that gives it life. If you feel that the devil is in control, bring love into your life. Colour also destroys darkness. Surround yourself with flowers and glowing colours, and the negative energies will retreat. Do not, under any circumstances, allow this energy to interfere with your life. You have invited it in with negative thoughts. You can eliminate it with positive thoughts of love for life. Your mind is the control tower, and you are the controller.

Visualisation: You are filled with hate for a person who has practically destroyed your life. The intense feelings fill your being and, as they do so, you are aware that you are no longer in control. Instead, the black energies are consuming you, and your mind feels like pulp. Everything around you has been drained of colour and looks dark and lifeless, and you realise that this is also happening to you. It is only then that you understand how like attracts like. With superhuman effort, you cancel the object of your hate with the colours of your mind. Gradually, you recall the feelings of love that you have experienced throughout your life. The struggle is hard and long, but inch by inch you can feel the black energies being banished and life-force flowing through your body, and you know that you will win this particular battle. You have learned the most valuable lesson of your life. Thoughts must always be disciplined. Emotions can never be stifled but neither can they be allowed to become obsessions.

Affirmation: I will fight the devil within for I have so much love to give.

47

❧

Discipline

The discipline of colleges and universities
is in general contrived,
not for the benefit of the students,
but for the interest, or more properly speaking,
for the ease of the masters.

SAMUEL SMILES
1812–1904

IT IS THE BREAKDOWN of discipline that leads to disaster. Yet too much discipline can also cause havoc, especially with the emotions. Parents are always asking themselves if they are giving too much or too little to their children. But there are guidelines. If your children are badly behaved in public then they are not receiving enough discipline at home. If they appear to be browbeaten then the discipline could be bordering on abuse. Happy, carefree children who have respect for their parents are more likely to be receiving moderate amounts of discipline intertwined with love. By monitoring your children's behaviour, you could also learn a lot about yourself.

Large organisations have to have rules, but individual discipline should also be encouraged to correct any problems. That way you have the best of both worlds.

Visualisation: **You are incensed by the actions of a particular individual, and violence is uppermost in your mind as you approach your antagonist. But somewhere in the depths of your subconscious you hear a voice saying, 'Don't do that!' The memory of your mother repeating that phrase makes you stop and think. You turn and walk away from the confrontation. The discipline received as a child is never forgotten.**

Affirmation: I will discipline with humour, which will lighten everyone's life.

48
❧

Discontent

And sigh that one thing only has been lent
To youth and age in common – discontent.

MATTHEW ARNOLD
1822–1888

IF YOU ARE CONSTANTLY discontented then you are under-achieving. That does not mean that you ought *never* to be discontented with your life – this would be an impossible target. But it does mean that whenever you feel that way, you should decide whether it can be altered. If not, you should move on to something more exciting, more interesting. If you are unable to do that then you must find an antidote. But please, do not stay discontented for any longer than you need. If you do, then matters will get worse. You have to make the effort – only you can make it work.

Visualisation: You are in a bad mood because nothing seems to be going right for you. Thinking about your work, relationship, financial position, does not make the situation better. As you mull these things over the molehills grow into mountains. A friend walks into the room, takes one look at you and says, 'Crikey! Things can't be that bad. For heaven's sake cheer up. You have your health and you can work.' Disgusted with your miserable attitude, he leaves the room. You feel ashamed. So many people are ill or without any means of support. Some of them are your friends, and yet you are more discontented than they are. You make a promise to yourself not to have such a chip on your shoulder again.

Affirmation: For heaven's sake, cheer up!

49
❧
Discretion

A good man is merciful, and lendeth:
and will guide his words with discretion.
For he shall never be moved: and the righteous
shall be had in everlasting remembrance.

PRAYER BOOK
1662

To BE DISCREET is to care, not to want to hurt unduly, and this can be extremely difficult if you have a spontaneous personality. The words are out before you have time to think about them. Anger is another occasion when indiscretion comes to the fore. What can you do about it? Practise thinking before you speak, write or act. It does help. When you are angry, try to keep quiet until you have calmed down. This is also extremely difficult, but do try. You never know, one day it may save you from something very nasty.

Visualisation: **You are out with a friend and you come face-to-face with her ex-husband. Because the divorce was bitter, she is extremely upset and avoids a confrontation with him. However, having supported her through a bad time, you are aching to read him the riot act. You open your mouth to speak, but at the last minute you change your mind and leave the scene, because in that split second you realise that you do not have the right to judge.**

If you believe in Universal Law, let that be the judge. If you do not believe, just be discreet, and have faith.

Affirmation: Discretion in all things.

50

❧

Dishonesty

Not the owner of many possessions will you be
right to call happy: he more rightly deserves
the name of happy who knows how to use the gods'
gifts wisely and to put up with rough poverty, and who fears
dishonour more than death.

HORACE
65–8 BC

To BE DISHONEST is to be a traitor to that great gift, the mind. There are so many ways to acquire what you most desire in life rather than stooping to dishonesty. It usually begins in childhood. Either the parents turn a blind eye, not wishing to face the fact that their child is showing dishonest tendencies, or they are oblivious of the fact, and the child gets away with it. Either way, once it starts it is very difficult to stop and the child will grow up with the notion that everything and everybody can be controlled by their dishonesty.

This problem can sometimes lie dormant until later in life, but even as adults guilt is never part of the make-up of dishonest characters, so the person who tries appealing to their better nature might find it difficult.

However, dishonest people have been known to reform when their problem has caused severe pain to someone they love, so there is always hope.

Visualisation: **You have been given the opportunity to be up-graded at work. But you know from previous experience that if you make false accusations against a fellow worker, your chances will be even better. So you lie. You have no guilt because you have been acting this way all your life and, what's more, have got away with it. You are the eternal optimist because you need to feel in control. Unfortunately, this time, you are found out. Not only do you lose your job but you will also leave without a reference. Was it worth it?**

Affirmation: I can reach my goals without being dishonest.

51

❦

Divorce

Seal then this bill of my Divorce to all.

JOHN DONNE
*c.*1571–1631

DIVORCE CAN BE a terrible thing. It can also be viewed as a positive opportunity. The two parties involved have that choice. If the relationship is over, albeit perhaps from only one side's perspective, it *is* over. Seek out an experienced solicitor, who will help you to solve the many problems that come with divorce settlements, and who is sympathetic to both individuals. It can be done and consequently you can remain friends and help each other over the difficult transition. This is the brighter side of the coin. But divorce is a minefield for most people, and if they choose to fight, squabble and abuse each other, the health of both of them will, most definitely, suffer. There are so many stresses in our everyday existence that the addition of a hateful divorce can be the last straw. Through people who have come to me for healing, I have seen the end results and they are often tragic.

Bitterness is usually part and parcel of a divorce but, if you can, keep this within your friends and family. Of course you want to rant and rave, and it will probably keep you sane. But it is best kept apart from the legal wrangle. It rarely solves anything and strangers will never understand your anguish. Only your nearest and dearest can help you with that.

Visualisation: **You are ranting and raving and calling your partner all the names under the sun. Your friends are giving you sympathy, tea and biscuits. They are there for you. You decide to go for everything you can get in the settlement because you feel that is the only way to control the bitterness inside you. Unfortunately, that same bitterness is carving your body up into small pieces and spitting them out in the form of headaches, mental trauma, bowel disorders, and much more. You decide to be content with the outcome, whatever it may be. Your health recovers, and you know that there will be better times ahead, possibly with someone new. There is always a future, but if your health is in tatters happiness will be more difficult to find.**

Affirmation: If there has to be divorce, then I will come out of it with my sanity and my health.

52

❧

Ego

*For the sake of a few fine imaginative
or domestic passages, are we to be bullied into a
certain philosophy engendered in the whims of an egoist.*

JOHN KEATS
1795–1821

EGO IS OKAY if you use it in the correct manner. Anyone who is in the public eye must have an ego if they want to impress the public. But the public is not impressed with that person if their ego is inflated. They become a target for the media and satirists and usually end up a laughing stock. Family members and friends become disenchanted and bored to death with the egoist. So, if you have an over-inflated ego and are puffed up with your own self-importance, then do something about it. The best way to do this is to ask a friend to make a video of a 'day in the life of' and study it. Or look at the faces around you whilst you are expounding your theories or 'doing your stuff'. I think you will be surprised. Egotism is curable but takes effort. Are you going to make that effort? You might be surprised to find that you make many more friends.

Visualisation: **You are spending the day with an actor who cannot stop performing. His ego is such that he really believes that he is the only one in the cast of his current assignment who has given a fantastic performance and that, without him, all would have been lost. Even worse, he is a terrible bore. Unfortunately, he is a mirror image of yourself. As this realisation gradually dawns on you, the humiliation is unbearable. You understand now why you have lost friends, and why you have made so many enemies. Understanding is the beginning. Adding humility to your character can bring about a happy ending.**

Affirmation: Egocentric personalities are a bore.

53

❧

Embarrassment

Jack was embarrassed – never hero more,
And as he knew not what to say, he swore.

LORD BYRON
1788–1824

YOU WOULD BE a very lucky person indeed if you had never embarrassed someone or experienced embarrassment yourself. It is all part and parcel of life. Every time this happens to you, just tell yourself that you are not alone in the world, that there are hundreds of people suffering the same agonies at that very moment. You are not unique. However, if you are in the *habit* of causing embarrassment to others, then now is the time to stop. You may be getting a good laugh out of it, but you know that if the tables were turned you would be very angry indeed. So don't be selfish. If the joke cannot be shared in fun by all concerned, then don't do it.

The main cause of embarrassment is shyness, and it is a real problem. If this applies to you, then always choose your friends and partners carefully to avoid further unease. Shyness can be alleviated if you are able to laugh at yourself.

Visualisation: You have been the victim of a hoax, and are angry that you have allowed yourself to be taken in. As the tears well up in your eyes you are terrified that your emotions will cause even further embarrassment. With enormous effort you begin to laugh and, as you do, so the atmosphere changes and the hoaxers join in. Later, one of them takes you to one side and confides that you were the victim of the hoax because they believed that you had no sense of humour. Laughter can change everything. It is a great healer.

Affirmation: Laugh and the world laughs with you. Weep and you weep alone.

54

❦

Emotion

*Poetry is the spontaneous overflow of
powerful feelings:
it takes its origin from emotion recollected
in tranquillity.*

WILLIAM WORDSWORTH
1770–1850

OUR EMOTIONAL REACTIONS to situations throughout life are triggered by previous experiences. A look, word or action can bring to the surface both happy and unhappy memories and the response can sometimes be quite unexpected and mystifying, even to ourselves. It is a good idea to try to bring all of your emotions to the fore, either by writing them all down as they occur or discussing them with a friend. Friends that you can trust with your life are rare, but if you are lucky and have such a friend, then talk to them. Get it all out into the open. Whatever you do, do not allow negative emotions to fester, for they will surface again when you least expect it.

Being over-emotional *all* the time will, without doubt, have a devastating effect on your health. It causes havoc with the immune system, so beware!

Visualisation: You are having a conversation with your son and daughter, who are now parents themselves, and you ask them what their most embarrassing moments were when they were small. They laugh, and tell you that your over-emotional response to their childhood problems had been the greatest embarrassment. 'We know how much you loved us, Mum,' your daughter says, 'but you were so over the top.'

Your son interrupts her, saying, 'In a way it helped me, because I recognised the signs when I started over-reacting to my own children's problems. From my own experience I knew that they needed both. Lots of loved mixed with splashes of logic and common sense.'

When they have finished speaking they are afraid that they have said too much, that you will be annoyed at their criticism, and are surprised when you say, 'You're right. I think we all learned from my mistakes.'

If you keep making the same mistakes over and over, then now is the time to take stock and learn from them. Don't let them happen again. You will be doing yourself and others a great favour. There are only so many times a friend can pick up the same old pieces and put you together again.

Affirmation: My emotions are part and parcel of my being, but they must be controlled.

55

❧

Encouragement

I wish you all the joy that you can wish.

WILLIAM SHAKESPEARE
1564–1616

IF YOU ARE GIVEN ENCOURAGEMENT from family, teachers and friends from an early age, then you are more likely to be successful in later life than those who received little or no encouragement at all. There are exceptions, and these are the people who are determined to prove themselves, come what may. They are made of sterner stuff than the majority. I am a great believer in the fact that anything and everything is possible. However, those who carry a chip on their shoulders because of the lack of support in their childhood may make it to the top, but their success is usually marred by negative memories invading their perception at crucial times, which affects their ability to judge difficult situations fairly. If you recognise this failing you will find the following visualisation helpful.

Visualisation: You are the owner of a large company. You received no encouragement as a child, and your present success is a result of your own abilities. In your employ you have clever and competent staff who seem to fall into two groups: some have made it the hard way, while others have had all the encouragement and help they needed. During one of your meetings, a heated argument breaks out between two of your staff. One of them is from the former group, the other from the latter. You allow them to argue whilst you make an assessment. Unfortunately, the underlying resentment due to lack of encouragement in your youth comes to the fore, and you are about to favour the person with a similar background to yourself. Then the experience you have acquired over the years overcomes the prejudice. You ask them to repeat their accusations slowly and quietly, then you make a fair judgement.

Later, when you are alone, you realise that the chip you have been carrying around for so long is no longer there, and you resolve to bury your prejudices for ever.

Affirmation: I will give encouragement wherever it is needed.

56

Energy

Energy is Eternal Delight.

WILLIAM BLAKE
1757–1827

M Y ABILITY TO STUDY ENERGIES clairvoyantly has given me an insight into the minds of all living things.

We are energy beings first and foremost. Without our energy counterpart of the physical body, we would not be here at this moment. But stress causes energy blockages in the physical system causing distress and dis-ease.

Do not underestimate the power of the mind. It is the mind that first of all gives birth to the thought – both positive and negative. It created the atom bomb, and has been the cause of all the destructive elements around the world. That is the negative side. The positive side is that it also creates the beautiful things in the world. It is the creator of great art and counteracts the negative energies which would otherwise take over the world. It makes waves – waves of love, compassion and understanding – and it heals.

Visualisation: **You have been made aware that a relative living abroad has become very ill. As you have not spoken for many years you feel unable to write or phone. However, you know the power of positive thought and send loving thoughts to the patient. Every day, at the same hour, your love is formed by thought and sent along the energy network that surrounds the globe to reach its destination.**

Three weeks have passed and you begin to wonder whether your healing thoughts reached their destination. Then you receive a letter from the patient, which says, 'I know that we have not spoken for some time, but every day I can see your face, smiling at me. I wonder why? Although I have been quite ill, the doctor has been amazed at my rapid recovery. My illness has made me aware of how stupid it is for us not to be friends. Please write.'

Why not try giving healing to someone in need and make use of the incredible energies that surround us and give us life?

Affirmation: Energy is life. Life is fantastic.

57

❧

Entertaining

Lay aside life-harming heaviness,
And entertain a cheerful disposition.

WILLIAM SHAKESPEARE
1564–1616

To BE ENTERTAINING depends entirely on whether or not you like the company you are in. If you are the host or hostess, having to entertain someone you dislike can be a nightmare. Unfortunately, in business you are expected to be nice to everyone.

In your private life it is wise not to mix too many personalities when it is your turn to play host. Those whom you do choose must have at least one common interest. If you can achieve this, then entertaining will be a pleasure. But life is far from ideal and, inevitably, there will be times when you will have to entertain someone with whom you are incompatible.

You may ask why? Why *should* you make the effort to be pleasant when your instincts are giving you a different message? Why not be honest and act accordingly? It is because it is selfish to spoil it for the other guests. Whether it is a lunch, a dinner, a party or just a small gathering of people, and whether you are the host or a guest, it is good manners to make it a successful occasion for all concerned.

Visualisation: **You have been asked to attend a business dinner. Taking time over your appearance, you arrive at your destination. As you enter, you take in the pleasant atmosphere and join in. Midway through a conversation with a colleague you recognise someone who, in the past, has made life unbearable for you. Making your excuses, you disappear outside for a moment and contemplate whether to stay or leave. If you stay you will have to be pleasant to someone you dislike intensely. If you leave you will upset your colleagues. You have no choice. Good manners must prevail, so you rejoin the party.**

Affirmation: Good manners must always prevail.

58
❧

Envy

If at times my eyes are lenses
through which the brain explores
constellations of feeling
my ears yielding like swinging doors
admit princes to the corridors
into the mind, do not envy me.
I have a beast on my back.

KEITH DOUGLAS
1920–1944

ENVY CAN POISON the mind and corrupt the soul, causing disruptive behaviour, violence and death. Every day there is evidence of the evil that it brings into our lives, and the tragedy is that it can start in childhood. Never covet this emotion – it can lead only to disaster.

I have met thousands of people who appear to have everything but, like everyone else in this world, they still have to spend their time surviving. Bad luck can hit us when we least expect it, whether we are rich or poor. If you have an envious nature, then friends will be thin on the ground. This leads to loneliness which in turn gives rise to bitterness. Do not allow it to enter your mind or your heart. Fight it!

Visualisation: Touring the area in which you live, you become envious of the big houses that are scattered around. You feel that you would give your soul to live in one of them, to have that kind of status. Turning a corner, you pass a mansion. A long winding drive set in the centre of a landscaped garden leads to the front door, and as you watch the door opens, and a nurse pushing a wheelchair walks down the drive. On impulse, you get out of the car and speak to the occupant of the wheelchair, a man in his fifties. 'I hope you don't mind, I was just admiring your house.'

The man smiles, 'There's no harm in admiring it,' he says, 'but don't envy the owner. I have been crippled for years. Can't even walk the grounds.' He points to a neighbour's house, of the same quality as his own. 'I am just going to visit my friend next door. He has lost his son in a car crash.' You bid him goodbye.

On the drive back home you ponder on the tragedies of those two families, tragedies that will have affected not only close family, but also relatives and friends. Later, when you walk through your own front door, you realise how lucky you are to have a happy, healthy family and vow never to feel envious again.

Affirmation: I will not envy others. A healthy, happy nature is worth its weight in gold.

59

✤

Excess

The best things carried to excess are wrong.

CHARLES CHURCHILL
1731–1764

IF YOU LOVE SOMETHING or someone, you will – simply because you are a human being – take things to excess. This behaviour is understandable, but it is not healthy if it continues. Self-satisfaction can become habitual and will eventually lead to your downfall, emotionally, financially, or in health. Excess can only be tolerated a little at a time. For your own sake you must know when to slow down or stop.

Visualisation: You have been quarrelling with a neighbour for over a year. This has caused unhappiness in both households, and yet neither will give way and try to heal the rift. It is obvious to friends that the outcome could become violent, but neither of you will heed the warnings; that is, until your children show the first signs of violent behaviour. Realising that they are only mimicking the adults, you both decide to apologise and end the arguments. Through an intelligent approach to the problems, peace is restored. But it could so easily have been a different story.

Affirmation: Excessive behaviour can lead to disaster. Be careful!

60

❧

Expectations

What we anticipate seldom occurs;
what we least expected generally happens.

BENJAMIN DISRAELI
1804–1881

EXPECTATIONS are the main cause of unhappiness in life – expectancy of reward, perfect relationships, perfect children, perfect life. Forget it! It will never happen. The best you can hope for is to be treated with the respect you deserve, meaning that whatever you give out will come back. Being optimistic, you could receive more than you give, and that's a bonus. But do not fall into the trap of raised expectancy because it can only bring unhappiness. Human beings are imperfect, and that is why you must make all the wonderful things happen for yourself.

Do not rely on others for your happiness. If a partner or a friend adds to the experience, then that is wonderful, but do not make them the be-all and end-all of your life. You must be in control at all times. If you let yourself down then you only have yourself to blame. Do not allow others to run your life. If you are in control you will find life more enjoyable.

Stop having expectations. Make your life work for you by accepting it as it is for the moment, and work toward your future dreams with light, love and laughter, for they are the jewels of life.

Visualisation: **You are surrounded by friends. The room is full of light, love and laughter. Suddenly, the whole atmosphere changes. A small group is trying to steal the limelight, talking about achievements and expectancy of reward. Others walk away and sit in the corner of the room. They are smiling, holding hands and supporting each other, and you know they are the kind of friends that you need if you want to succeed.**

Affirmation: I will not have expectations of others. I will make it happen for myself.

61

❧

Extra-sensory perception

When my love swears that she is made of truth,
I do believe her, though I know she lies.

WILLIAM SHAKESPEARE
1564–1616

YOU DO NOT HAVE TO BE psychic to have extra-sensory perception. It is an integral part of your spiritual energy – your mind. You may not be very perceptive physically, but extra-sensory perception does not work in this dimension. If you are a giver and are positive, then the mind expands and touches the energy dimension which sparks off the 'knowing' factor, the sense of right and wrong. The effect is immediate and makes waves through the whole of your psyche. Don't argue with it, but learn from it.

Visualisation: You decide to take a walk through the woods near your home. Turning right on to an overgrown path you become aware of a seemingly unfounded fear. Whilst trying to decide whether you should heed this negative feeling, you realise that you can hear the loud beating of your heart and your fear is growing. You retrace your steps. Later in the day you are told that a young woman had been attacked there by a man and he was still prowling the area.

Affirmation: I will heed my senses and act accordingly.

62

❧

Faith

*Faith consists in believing when it is
beyond the power of reason to believe. It is not
enough that a thing be possible for it to be believed.*

VOLTAIRE
1694–1778

IT IS ALMOST IMPOSSIBLE if you have an analytical mind to have faith. Faith requires absolute belief in something which is beyond your control. Yet, through healing, I have seen the analysts-cum-sceptics do a complete U-turn and become believers in a power that has no scientific explanation.

Having faith in something good brings an added dimension to your life. Having faith in yourself is even better.

Visualisation: You are going through a black period in your life. You have split with friends and family and have lost your job. While out walking one day, you see a small isolated church and decide to go in and look around. Although religion has not played any real part in your life, you have always been interested in the churches themselves, not just for the architecture, but for the peaceful atmosphere and, when empty, the beauty of silence. As you look around now, you sense something else, that somewhere in this building there is an energy that heals. It wraps itself around you like a warm blanket and, in that moment, you know that you are not alone, that someone cares. As you close your eyes to receive this gift, you are made aware of that part of your personality that has brought you to these depths, and you cry. As the tears fall and you are cleansed, you can feel all the anger, bitterness and self-pity leave, and you promise yourself that whatever you achieve in life it will not be to the disadvantage of others. You have lost so many friends. Now is the time to renew those friendships and to make new ones.

Affirmation: I will have faith in the good of others and belief in myself.

63

❧

Fame

What is fame? an empty bubble;
Gold? a transient, shining trouble.

JAMES GRAINGER
*c.*1721–1766

THE HIGHS AND LOWS of fame are legendary. Do you want your life to be invaded by the media? Do you need a dozen houses around the world? (You can only live in one at a time.) Do you need five cars when only one would suffice? Do you want to get up in the morning and see a photograph of yourself looking like death in the morning paper? Or someone pulling you to pieces on television? Do you want to have to look behind you for the rest of your life for the shadow of someone who will be next in line for your job or status? If you do, then go ahead, seek the fame that you so desire. Sure, you will also have money, but acquiring it becomes addictive and you will end up selling yourself to the highest bidder. As for the tax man, he will be your constant companion.

I know all this because I have treated hundreds of famous people. I know the stories of their lives. They, and their families, have paid a high price for their fame. Well-meaning, hard-working, they fought their way to the top. Yes, they have money, but the broken relationships, loss of real friends, and their mistrust of everyone, has not been worth it. Fame gives, but it also takes in mighty chunks, especially your health. Fame is an empty vessel.

Instead of seeking fame, why not simply enjoy your talent and your friends? If you are that good, fame will meet you half-way. So many deluded people waste their lives trying to exploit a talent that is moderate instead of living life to the full. Give yourself a chance to find the real you.

Visualisation: You are famous. Everyone seeks your opinion. You travel the world sampling the delights you dreamed of for so many years. But you rarely see your wife and children, and when you return for a short break you realise that you are now a stranger to them and can feel the hostility emanating from them. Remembering how happy you all were before you became famous, you realise that nothing can replace the warmth of a loving family. You ring your agent and instruct him to cut your work-load by half. He isn't happy, but you are. The taste of honey, you have found, is much better in small spoonfuls.

Affirmation: Fame is an empty vessel. Only I can decide what it will contain.

64

❧

Familiarity

Yea, even mine own familiar friend, whom I trusted:
who did also eat of my bread, hath laid great wait for me.

PRAYER BOOK
1662

FAMILIARITY BREEDS CONTEMPT. We hear this phrase time and again but rarely think about it. Yet it is so true. Friends and family alike seem to think that they can be contemptuous of your friends, your success, and most of all your free will, and that you won't mind. Everyone should be treated with respect. Shared, intimate thoughts and moments should be sacred, and promises of confidentiality kept. If you are not sure whether you can trust someone, then do not open yourself up to them; keep quiet until they have proved themselves. Only time will tell.

Having friends and family with whom you can be familiar is a different thing altogether. It gives a feeling of belonging, of love, of giving and receiving, of knowing that you are an important part of the whole. It is, above all, a warm, cosy feeling, like warming your toes by the fire. Familiarity in this sense is worth more than its weight in gold.

The following exercise is to benefit those for whom familiarity does breed contempt.

Visualisation: **Having spent the day with a close friend listening to her intimate stories, you promise not to abuse that friendship and to keep the information confidential. But when you leave, you forget your promise and during the next two days you pass on all that you have learnt. As usual, what goes around comes around, and the friend you have so badly let down accuses you of being a Judas. As she walks away from you, you cannot forget the look of disdain and hurt on her face. Over the next few weeks, those that listened to you also walk away, because they have realised that you cannot be trusted with a secret. You are going to pay a high price for your indiscretion.**

Affirmation: Familiarity can breed contempt, or it can be a blessing. Only I can decide.

65

❧

Fatigue

Thinking is to me the greatest fatigue in the world.

SIR JOHN VANBRUGH
1664–1726

IT IS VERY DIFFICULT to diagnose the cause of fatigue, because the symptoms can be related to minor or major medical problems. If you have been feeling fatigued for some time, then consult a doctor.

However, there is an excellent way of dealing with non-clinical fatigue, and that is with meditation, or just day-dreaming. Either way, you take the pressure of the mind energy off the brain and body, which removes energy blockages throughout the body, resulting in the rejuvenation of the whole system. Problems will never again take over your life. The added perception you will gain with meditation enables you to find corners of your mind where you can tuck away the things that threaten to overwhelm you until you can deal with them intelligently. Give your mind and your body a break!

Visualisation: **You are sitting on a balcony overlooking the Pacific Ocean. Coasters are rolling in, and the sound of the waves lulls you into a meditative state. The sun is warm and relaxing. A feeling of weightlessness engulfs you and you become as one with the universe. When you awake you feel as though all your problems have been resolved. Practise every day.**

Affirmation: Meditation every day keeps fatigue away.

66

❧

Favouritism

*I have lived long enough in the world
to see that necessity is a bad recommendation to favours . . .
which as seldom fall to those who really want them, as to
those who really deserve them.*

HENRY FIELDING
1707–1754

FAVOURITISM IS GENERALLY UNFAIR. It is wonderful to be the flavour of the month but pretty lousy to be the one on the outside. Even if you are the favourite, for whatever reason, you will find that there is a price – that price is freedom of thought, word and deed, and in the end you will have to pay it. It is far better to reach your goals with talent and without favour. The only positive kind of favour is that which is given without expectancy of reward.

Visualisation: **You are a popular figure at your place of work. But deep down you know that because of your amiable nature you have always attracted favouritism, and dealing with it has brought you much grief. You are not your own person, and you are sick of always trying to pretend to be something you are not and please others. Accusations of unfairness are always being voiced. You decide you have had enough, and the next time someone tries to make you their favourite you are going to decline. It is better to learn this sooner than later. Remember, you always have to pay for the privilege.**

Affirmation: Favouritism is wrong. Everyone should be equal.

67

❦

Fear

*Let me assert my firm belief that the
only thing we have to fear is fear itself.*

PRESIDENT FRANKLIN D. ROOSEVELT
1882–1945

FEAR IS DESTRUCTIVE. It eats into our soul and disables constructive thought. Yet there is so much to fear in the world today that violence and the negative actions of others can paralyse our lives. But we have to deal with it, the same as we have to deal with ordinary, everyday fears, like ridding our homes of insects and spiders that fill many of us with dread. We have to face our worst fears, and then think them through to a positive end result. Then, if we are faced with that particular situation again, we will know exactly what to do. If we treat all our fears in this way, we will be taking control of our own lives, and this positive attitude will strengthen our resolve to banish fear from our lives.

Visualisation: You are constantly afraid of being alone in the house, and decide to do something about it. Sitting down in a comfortable chair, you act out the fear. Through this exercise you realise that you have not done everything possible to make your home safe. You seek help from the experts at your local police station. They advise you and, taking that advice, you make your home more secure. The fears gradually subside.

You can modify this visualisation to any fear you have. Relive it, rationalise it, decide how to lessen the horrors and who best can help you to overcome them in a practical way.

Affirmation: I must take positive action and face my fears.

68

❧

Forgiveness

We read that we ought to forgive our enemies;
but we do not read that we ought to forgive our friends.

COSIMO DE' MEDICI
1389–1464

I T IS VERY DIFFICULT to forgive, especially if the perpetrator of the crime appears to escape punishment. It is human nature for you to want them to suffer as you have done. But if you hang on to all the anguish received throughout your life, you are the one who is going to feel it most. The human spirit can only take so much. Far better to let go and let Universal Law take over. Everything is known, and at some time everyone will have to face the crimes they have committed against humanity, either here or in another dimension. I have seen retribution meted out from extremely unexpected sources just a few days after an unpleasant incident, and it is always when the person responsible for the action is at their lowest ebb, so it affords the maximum effect.

One has only to study the results of the hatred that runs through communities around the world to see negative energies at their most devastating. And this terrible animosity is passed on through the generations.

If you are holding on to negative feelings, get rid of them now and be an example to those around you. If you cannot forgive, then move on. There is always life after sorrow. Live and let live.

Visualisation: **Black clouds of hatred are consuming your being. You have been deceived by someone whom you thought was a trusted friend. Images of all the things you would like to happen to them tumble through your mind. Consumed with anger, you plan your revenge.**

Two weeks later, you are suffering pains in the chest and are unable to breathe. You consult your doctor. After various tests and consultations he tells you that your ailments are the end result of continued stress, and that whatever is causing it must go.

Three weeks later, having written down on paper – and later reduced to ashes – all the grievances you had held for so long, you find that the hatred has been replaced by charity and a more positive attitude. The time has been well spent.

Affirmation: My health must come first. If I cannot forgive and forget, I must move on.

69

✤

Fun

Fun is fun but no girl wants to laugh all of the time.

ANITA LOOS
1893–1981

I BELIEVE WE HAVE the most fun when there are no strings attached. When you have the time to please yourself and not have to worry about anyone else. You can still have fun with someone special, but you have to feel so at ease with them that they feel a part of you. Fun is usually something you have when there is a rapport within a group of people and there is a lot of leg-pulling and much laughter.

Fun is something that we all need in abundance, so look for it wherever and whenever you can.

Visualisation: Picture yourself going out with a party of friends. You are laughing and joking, and you can feel all the tension leaving your mind and body. This freedom is a sensation that has been missing from your life for too long. You promise yourself that in future the 'fun' times will not be so few and far between.

Affirmation: To release the tensions I am going to have fun, fun and more fun.

70

❧

Gifts

*Every good gift and every perfect gift is from above,
cometh down from the Father of lights, with whom
is no variableness neither shadow of turning.*

THE BIBLE, JAMES

IF YOU HAVE BEEN BORN with gifts, do not waste them. They are a blessed mixture of all the things you have acquired in past lives, born out of hard work and courage. They are your birthright. Work at them, add to them, and you will join like-minds and fulfil the expectations of your spiritual tutors, who are always there, watching, encouraging, and giving a helping hand when things get tough. It is at these times that you must also remember that the more difficult a situation becomes, the more character-building it is. The bonus is that this leads to freedom of expression and independence. It will be worth it.

Visualisation: Your dancing teacher has taken you through the same dancing routine six times. You are tired and irritable and are about to voice your opinions and pack up, when he suddenly informs you that he is giving you the most coveted role in a musical. As you are leaving, he says, 'I know what you were thinking; remember, I went through the same agonies when I was young.' With a knowing smile, he adds, 'you were wise to keep quiet, and not to give up. Nobody likes a quitter.'

Affirmation: I will not quit.

71

Giving

I am not in the giving vein today.

WILLIAM SHAKESPEARE
1564–1616

No MATTER HOW GENEROUS you may be, it is understandable to have days when you are not in the giving vein. If you are a born giver, then inevitably the takers will latch on to you throughout your life. The secret is to know when to stop giving. This will only come through experience, and even then it is difficult. Try to strengthen your mind so that it becomes easier to say 'No'.

Visualisation: **You are being asked to give advice to an acquaintance who has persistently ignored your previous attempts at solving her problems. As you are about to give in to her request, a big NO imprints itself on your mind, and you make your excuses and leave. This refusal is the result of all the mental exercises that you had set yourself whilst having a quiet moment. Have faith in your higher mind. It will never let you down.**

Affirmation: *'No' must become a regular part of my vocabulary.*

72

❦

Gratitude

*One single grateful thought raised to heaven
is the most perfect prayer.*

G. E. LESSING
1729–1781

A T SOME TIME in your life I am sure you will have had reason to be grateful to someone and will have given thanks for their help. Is there a danger, however, that the character of the helper wants and needs you to be forever grateful to boost their ego? If so, perhaps you should refuse their offer of help and seek it elsewhere. They should assist without expectancy of reward. The receiver can always give a verbal thanks (and perhaps a silent thanks to the power that brought it about), and that should be the end of the gratitude. Positive thought and perhaps the opportunity to return the favour can be withheld until such a time that it can be returned without obligation.

Visualisation: In your time of need, someone has come to your aid and thus averted a financial disaster. You give thanks, and assure the benefactor that you will return the money when it is possible to do so. However, he reminds you of the favour every time you meet, and this inevitably affects your health. Eventually you pay back the debt, and vow never again to accept help from that particular source.

Despite the ill-feeling, you are reassured that this situation has also strengthened your resolve to pay more attention to your finances in the future.

Affirmation: I will refuse help from anyone who seeks to back up their inferiority or boost their ego by giving favours.

73

❧

Greed

*You cannot hope
to bribe or twist,
thank God! the
British journalist.*

*But, seeing what
the man will do
unbribed, there's
no occasion to.*

HUMBERT WOLFE
1886–1940

I HAVE SEEN at close hand what people will do for money and fame. Unleashed greed is dangerous and drags everyone concerned into a web of lies, deceit, and the destruction of innocent individuals. This kind of behaviour gives birth to criminal tendencies which, if not curbed at the outset, will become habitual and arrive at a point of no return.

If you have greed in your heart, then there is something seriously wrong with your spiritual values. This has very little to do with religion. It is what you make of the spiritual energy that is your mind that enables you to claim spirituality. You should commit yourself to attain goals that will take you on the path of progression.

Of course, if you *are* a greedy person you are likely to ignore these words. Well, no one is perfect, but do try to be less selfish and to give a little.

Visualisation: You have been offered a great deal of money to do something that is illegal. Not having any previous experience of wrong-doing you hesitate, but your greed overrules the warning messages that you are receiving from your higher mind. You will do it. But you are caught and it leads to a prison sentence. Was it really worth it?

Affirmation: I may not be rich but I'm happy.

74

Grief

Farewell sadness
Good day sadness
You are inscribed in the lines of the ceiling.

PAUL ÉLUARD
1895–1952

TEARS SHED BY THOSE who are grieving are the only blessed relief when you are locked in an anguished embrace of memories of things that were meant to be and words that were never said.

There is no set time when you should relinquish the cloak of despair and 'look to the future'. You can only do that when the time is right, and because we are all unique, this time period will be different for everyone. It is the act of grieving that, when burnt out, will bring its own kind of peace. And again, as unique beings, it will be an original experience.

At these times we need our nearest and dearest. If you are alone, ask for help, if not from someone close then from one of the many organisations that are full of caring people. Do not go through a grieving period alone.

Visualisation: You have just lost a loved one and are sitting alone. Memories of what has been, and dreams of what might have been, crowd in and tears begin to flow. Pain surges through your heart and the grief becomes unbearable. Then you remember the words of a friend, 'If you are ever in need contact me, night or day.' You pick up the phone and speak to her. Within minutes she is knocking at your door and holding you tight, and the pain is easier to bear.

Affirmation: Ask and I will receive.

75

❧

Grievance

*Every time I make an appointment, I make one
ungrateful person and a hundred with a grievance.*

LOUIS XIV
1638–1715

WHEN GRIEVANCES TAKE OVER your mind, logical thought becomes impossible. Holding a grievance, whether valid or not, is a great time waster and will affect your health, because the poison darts of thought will travel and return ten-fold. I am quite sure that if you have deliberately turned to this page, you do not want this kind of clear-sighted advice. When you are holding a grudge all you want to hear is other people backing and strengthening your allegations. However, please read these words and think about them. If not, you will be the loser.

Visualisation: You are outraged by the cruel act of a friend. It does not affect you personally, but the loyalty you feel towards the person who has been harmed causes you to take up the cudgels on their behalf. It is you who writes the vindictive letters, you who makes the accusing telephone calls and you who spreads the gossip. At first, you feel great. Justice has been seen to be done.

A few weeks later your energy levels have sunk so low that you are too fatigued to carry out your normal everyday tasks, and you realise, as the electric currents vibrate through your body, that the adrenaline is still flowing but your system is unable to deal with the excess. Whilst you were going full blast you were using it up, but now that you have relaxed, it is causing adrenaline fatigue.

There are several ways you can deal with this, for deal with it you must if you do not want it to continue. Exercise is essential, as is rest. And meditation a must.

Next time you harbour a grievance, write it down, then destroy it.

Affirmation: Grievances can only lead to mental, physical and spiritual instability.

76

Guidance

Shall then this verse to future age pretend
Thou wert my guide, philosopher, and friend?
That urg'd by thee, I turn'd the tuneful art
From sounds to things, from fancy to the heart;
For wit's false mirror held up nature's light;
Shew'd erring pride, whatever is, is right;
That reason, passion, answer one great aim;
That true self-love and social are the same;
That virtue only makes our bliss below;
And all our knowledge is, ourselves to know.

ALEXANDER POPE
1688–1744

FROM BIRTH to the end of our lives we receive guidance from one source or another. The real test is whether you can separate the wheat from the chaff. The best way to do this is to absorb everything you are being told, and then spend ten minutes a day evaluating the information and sending whatever does not apply at that particular time in your life to your mental 'look at later' file.

Sometimes, what appears to be chaff will save you from yourself. Retain, separate and file. In time, what is of real worth will be recognised for what it is.

Visualisation: **Listening to guidance that you have sought, you are tempted to tell the counsellor that you believe his words are rubbish. Being a sensitive person, he is well aware of your thoughts but keeps going. When he has finished he asks you not to ignore his advice out of hand. 'If you go away and think about what I have said,' he says, 'it will make sense.' Later that day, when you are alone, memories of that session are revived. You realise, by breaking it down, that taking some of the advice would be beneficial to your life at that time. The parts that wouldn't, you file away. Two months later, when you are in need again, you are able to extract the file from memory and use the saved information.**

Guidance should be used as a stepping stone to independence and logical thought.

Affirmation: Listen, use, save: the reward is logical, independent thought.

⤬

77

Guilt

There is nothing either good or bad,
but thinking makes it so.

WILLIAM SHAKESPEARE
1564–1616

IF YOU ARE FEELING GUILTY and are unable to forget your wrong-doing then you must, somehow, find a way of putting things right. If this is impossible, you have no choice but to forget the whole incident, for if you carry guilt around like a sack of coals then it will destroy you.

On the other hand, if someone is deliberately making you feel guilty and you feel that you are innocent, you must let them know what you are thinking and then forget it. Pass it over so that they can deal with their own problem and not put it on to your shoulders. If this person happens to be your boss and you do not want to lose your job, wait until you get home, get a pad and pen, and write down all of your grievances until you are sick of writing. Then reduce it to ashes.

I have seen so many lives destroyed by ineffective people who pass their baggage on to others. Be wary, and make sure that this is not happening to you.

Visualisation: **Your boss is, as usual, trying to pass the buck by blaming you for not having posted some very important letters. When you explain that it was impossible for you to post them as he had not signed them, he becomes very angry. 'Well, you should have made sure that I had signed them,' he says. In a quiet voice you remind him that he had failed to return from a luncheon appointment and he had not left a contact number.**

Be polite, stand your ground, and make the culprit deal with their own guilt – as you will have to do when it applies to yourself.

Affirmation: I will deal with my own guilt and make others deal with theirs.

78
❧

Halo

What, after all,
Is a halo? It's only one more thing to
keep clean.

CHRISTOPHER FRY
1907–

THOSE OF YOU who have read my earlier books will know that my discovery of mind energy happened when I saw a halo of pure white energy around the head. I studied this energy for twelve years before I wrote my first book *Mind to Mind*, and found that every thought we have affects this energy. When we are positive it expands outwards *ad infinitum*, and when depressed it caves in and presses on the brain, causing dysfunction and blockages throughout the whole of our energy counterpart and also the physical. Keep your 'halo' lively and expansive by practising the following exercise every day.

Visualisation: Project an image of your halo on to the screen of your mind and watch it going outward towards the stars, linking up with the centre of the universe.

Affirmation: I will think positive thoughts every day to keep depression at bay.

79

Harmony

The day becomes more solemn and serene
When noon is past – there is a harmony
In autumn, and a lustre in its sky,
Which through the summer is not heard or seen,
As if it could not be, as if it had not been!

PERCY BYSSHE SHELLEY
1792–1822

HARMONY IN YOUR LIFE is essential if you want to succeed. It will elevate your spirit and bring peace to every fibre of your being. If you cannot attain it in your work or home, try to find a secret place where you can relax, if only for a few minutes every day. If all fails, find a space in your mind and elevate your thoughts until you feel yourself harmonising with the cosmic forces, for in these hallowed spaces you *will* find your secret place. Seek and find.

Visualisation: **Close your eyes and picture yourself floating through the air. Jump on a cloud. Fly!**

Affirmation: I must bring harmony into my life. I will succeed.

80

❦

Hate

I hate and I love: why I do so you may well ask.
I do not know, but I feel it happen and am in agony.

CATULLUS
*c.*87–54 BC

To HATE OVER A PROLONGED period will cause pain and suffering only to yourself. Hatred attracts negative energy that destroys everything in its path. Though it is possible that this destruction could bring you a certain satisfaction, it is addictive, and the habit is very difficult to break. I have seen people so filled with hate that one can see the pain that is raking their mind and body simply by looking into their eyes.

It is natural, at some time, to feel a certain hatred toward someone who has caused you pain, but it cannot continue. There are boundaries that should not be crossed. The problem is, how do you know you have crossed them? The answer lies within yourself. Are you feeling ill? Do you have more headaches than usual? Are you, as a healthy individual, now crippled with aches and pains? Is your revenge wreaking havoc with your relationships? Are you becoming depressed and disagreeable? There are many questions you could ask yourself, so why don't you give yourself the third degree and ask whether it is worth all the misery. Why not just walk away? Believe me, there are no winners in this game.

Visualisation: **Planning your revenge on someone who has caused you much pain, you find the detailed plans keep your mind occupied for hours and the possible end result raises your spirits and keeps you on a high. Unfortunately, your negative thoughts during this period have attracted like thoughts, and unseen clouds of black destructive energy are now attacking your body. Over the next few days pains in your legs make it very difficult to walk, and headaches prevent you from reading and sleeping. Relationships are affected, and life is becoming unbearable. In retrospect, you realise that it all began when you decided on retribution and that it is not worth the agony. You turn your back on the problem and walk away. But it is two months before your health returns. It is easier to attract dis-ease than to cure it.**

Affirmation: Hatred will consume my being. I must allow the light to return.

81

❧

Heartbreak

The heart-break in the heart of things.

WILFRED GIBSON
1878–1962

IF YOU ARE SUFFERING heart-break as you read these words, you are not alone. Someone, somewhere, is going through the same agonies as yourself. You may or may not recover from the pain that threatens to carve your heart into little pieces, but one thing is certain: life still goes on and you will have to deal with it somehow.

Let me assure you that you have every right to scream, cry, wail, bang your fists against the door and sob in the arms of a friend. It will rid you of some of the searing pain and relieve tension. Do not add to your sorrow by holding on to the negative energies that are threatening to overwhelm you, for they will, at some time, burst forth. Keep your mind and body intact by releasing the grief as I have described above. Above all, do not suffer alone. Call a friend.

Visualisation: **Sitting alone, mourning the death of a partner, you suddenly begin to rant and rave and shout. Why? Why did it have to happen to you? Why did you have to be left alone? The telephone rings; it is a friend asking if you would like her company. As you sob over the line, she is made aware of your plight and promises to be with you in minutes. Arriving at your home, she holds your sobbing form in her arms and asks why you didn't let her know of your needs before they became too tough for you to handle? So why didn't you?**

Affirmation: When I need help, need to speak to a friend, need someone to hold me close, I only have to ask.

82
❧

Heaven & Hell

Of this blest man, let his just praise be given,
Heaven was in him, before he was in heaven.

IZAAK WALTON
1593–1683

I DO NOT BELIEVE that we go to Heaven or Hell. I believe that we make our own Heaven and Hell wherever we may be. It is a state of mind, created by the same mind energy that leaves and slips into another dimension when the physical body dies. Your thoughts control your state of mind, and with freedom of thought, word and deed you must take responsibility for those thoughts.

There are factors that affect our lives that are outside of our control. But we can determine how we react to outside influences. Make a habit of looking at past problems, their cause and effect, and at the way you have dealt with them. You will find a pattern emerging that will give you an insight into whether or not you are managing okay.

Visualisation: Whilst day-dreaming, you are given a mental picture of your state of mind. Chaos and confusion are depicted as rubbish falling through space, and it is piling up in your subconscious, only to be spewed out again when you are at your lowest ebb. Like a boomerang you go back and forth, collecting even more rubbish on the way. This is your Hell. But you decide to do something about it. The next time it all comes tumbling down, you redirect it into a rubbish skip and it is taken away, never to be seen again. Now you have a different picture; a shining light that is burning away the darkness, bringing joy and selfless love. It is called enlightenment. This is your Heaven.

Affirmation: Remove the rubbish and find a Heaven on Earth.

83

❧

Humour

*The most perfect humour and irony is generally
quite unconscious.*

SAMUEL BUTLER
1835–1902

THOSE WITH AN UNCONSCIOUS sense of humour bring with them an innocence that is rarely seen in society today, for it also portrays an incorrupt honesty of a bygone age. From birth our children are victims of the media; they see violent crimes depicted on television day and night, and the vibes affect small children, as well as adults, causing a permanent sense of foreboding.

To counteract this, humour should be at the very centre of every family circle. Children should be encouraged to laugh at themselves, and to see the funny side of every situation. Life, love and laughter should be your motto. Laughter is the beginning of all healing – without it we are lost.

Visualisation: **A group of children are looking at a television series which contains scenes of violence. One by one the children take on the vibes and they begin to fight. You switch the television off and bring out a box of games. Soon their aggression subsides and they are competing and laughing with each other. Order has been restored with a little common sense.**

Affirmation: Humour is wonderful. I am going to encourage more of it into my life.

84

❧

Hygiene

All clean and comfortable I sit down to write.

JOHN KEATS
1795–1821

TO BE HYGIENIC is to have respect not only for ourselves but for those around us. Cleanliness should be part of our everyday routine. But there are those who decide to ignore this simple task, offending everyone with whom they come into contact. This kind of disrespect is unforgivable. If they really need to live unhygienic lives then they should become hermits.

If you are thinking of opting out of your hygiene routine when you are tired or just plain lazy, then think of all the people you know who ignore theirs and remind yourself of the offence they give to those around them. You will soon change your mind.

Visualisation: A friend asks if he can stay with you until he can find alternative accommodation, and you are happy to oblige. However, a few days pass and you notice that he rarely has a shower or bath, and there is no sign of any clothes being washed. You gradually stretch the space between you when you meet, and go to bed early rather than spend an evening in the same room. Eventually the strain becomes too much and there is a confrontation. Your friend's excuse is that hygiene is not a big thing in his life. You ask him to leave. Thoroughly cleaning your home, you realise how dirty he had made you feel during this period.

Affirmation: Hygiene is the outer cleanliness that mirrors my inner being.

85

❦

Ignorance

I pity his ignorance and despise him.

CHARLES DICKENS
1812–1870

THERE IS NO EXCUSE for ignorance in these enlightened times. Every conceivable form of education is on offer in school and evening classes. Societies are always printing up dates of their particular interest, and libraries are stacked with books on every subject. Obviously there are those who are unable to retain or understand this knowledge, and they need special care and encouragement, but for the ordinary student there is no excuse other than laziness. Even this can be overcome once they have found a subject that intrigues them and they feel the excitement of the first flutter of passion and enthusiasm. Opening new doors is like walking around a strange planet, with so many wonderful things to investigate. Life will never be the same. Seeking knowledge leads to strange and mysterious happenings. You will never know until you have taken your first step.

There are many people who blight our lives by being ignorant. Insensitive, rude, shallow and superficial, they bruise everyone who displeases them, leaving behind a trail of broken spirits. They are unhappy people who can't bear to see others happy. That is why it is impossible to help them. They need to look seriously at their state of mind. I avoid them and suggest that you do the same. If you are honest and can admit that you are an ignorant person, then the following exercise is for you.

Visualisation: **You are at work, and the latest addition to the staff, a young girl of seventeen, walks past and gives you a smile. Obviously nervous, she accidentally knocks some papers from your desk. Angry, you hurl abuse at her; she apologises, but you are determined to embarrass her and continue the abuse. Shaken, she trembles and becomes incoherent, and you feel justice has been done.**

If you recognise yourself then do something about it, for people will despise you for ever if you don't.

Affirmation: Nobody is born unpleasant. It takes dedication – not something to be proud of.

86

❧

Impulsiveness

*May I ask whether these pleasing attentions
proceed from the impulse of the moment, or are the
result of previous study?*

JANE AUSTEN
1775–1817

IMPULSIVE BEHAVIOUR is expected in children, but when it becomes a habit in adults it is no longer amusing. Inevitably, the problems become insurmountable as family and friends continually pick up the pieces and repair the damage that it causes. Restraint is a word unknown to these people as they childishly go on their way; some are so irritatingly unaware that they really believe they are God's gift to humanity.

On the other hand, the kind of impulsiveness that occasionally exudes from someone when they are excited and enthusiastic can lighten up the lives of everyone concerned. It can be lovable, endearing and laughable. This is normal and, at times, an added pleasure to our daily existence.

Which category do you fit into?

Visualisation: **Whilst taking a walk, you begin to show off to your partner by rushing up to greet every dog you see. You throw your arms around one particular dog allowing it to nuzzle your face. The owners, taken by surprise, are amazed at your impulsive behaviour. They warn you to be careful, but you are too absorbed in your performance. The inevitable happens; you are bitten on the face and, in your pain, scream at the owner. Your partner is mortified. 'You cannot blame anyone other than yourself,' you are told. 'Animals, like humans, have their limits. Your stupidity is unforgivable.'**

Affirmation: I must control my impulsiveness – it wastes time and energy, and leads to sorrow.

87

✤

Inactivity

An active line on a walk moving freely, without goal.
A walk for a walk's sake.

PAUL KLEE
1879–1940

I WILL NOT REPEAT the everyday medical warnings about inactivity, because this is not a book that deals with medicine. But it *is* about people's goals. Perhaps you have become inactive through overweight, fatigue or illness or are just plain lazy. Join the club! Unfortunately you are likely to suffer with numerous ailments.

Think about the energy counterpart of your physical body; about the way it vibrates through the whole of your system, stimulating each and every organ and cell, giving you the health and strength needed to live your life to the full. To feel the benefit of this incredible power you must also do your bit by keeping it moving. If you don't exercise, then you are not giving your mind and body the best chance of survival.

If you have a staircase in your home, try going up and down more often than you need. This is fantastic exercise, and one that heart patients have to manage before they are allowed to go home after surgery. Walking is good. Let's face it, you are not competing with anyone, so do everything in your own time. Set your own goals – just a few more steps a day is all that is needed to get going.

If you have a medical condition that prevents you from exercising, then make sure that you move whatever parts you can to keep the blood – and the energy – circulating. Some part of your body has to be kept on the move every day.

Visualisation: **Lazing around the home, you surround yourself with junk food and alcohol and spend all your free time watching television. After wasting your money on non-essentials, you can't even afford to meet your friends for a drink. You develop one cold after another as your immune system sinks to an all-time low. You become depressed and your body aches as though you are being invaded by an unseen enemy. You are falling apart.**

A visit to the doctor doesn't help at all. He cannot find anything wrong with you. However, a surprise visit from a friend solves the problem. He was in the same state eighteen months ago. He drags you out and encourages you to start walking, and two weeks later, your aches and pains have disappeared, along with the colds and depression. Also, the added oxygen intake has stimulated positive thinking, and you begin to make plans for the future.

Affirmation: I must keep moving.

88

❧

Incompatibility

I long for the harmony of compatibility
but it is not to be.

BETTY SHINE

INCOMPATIBILITY WITH FAMILY, partner or business associates is hell. Striving to survive whilst someone constantly undermines your efforts is a major factor in nervous breakdowns and suicide attempts. I know, because I have been in this situation myself, and have had to hold the hands and heal thousands of patients whose lives have been affected in this way. This awful state is usually apparent at first sight to those people who are involved. But if finances, marriage, employers or any other factor means that you feel you must soldier on, then being the stalwart beings that we are, you try to grin and bear it – only there is not much grinning, just a constant aching in your heart until the matter is resolved by the parting of the ways. Only then can you begin to heal. Incompatibility breeds contempt.

Visualisation: Watching a figure disappear into the distance, you feel as though a heavy load has been lifted from your heart and mind. You know that, by choice, you will never see or speak to that person again, because you have managed to survive years of incompatibility until this God-given moment when you said goodbye, and you know that no power on Earth is going to persuade you to reopen the door that had led to such a hellish existence.

Affirmation: The future is my own and it will be full of laughter. I must never look back.

89

✢

Irritability

I have to put up with a lot,
to please the sensitive race of poets.

HORACE
65–8 BC

IRRITABILITY! What an unpleasant word that is, conjuring up bad vibes and unpleasant situations. And yet human beings are plagued with it, either from within themselves or from others. When it rears its ugly head, a previously happy atmosphere can change to misery in minutes and the perpetrator isn't happy either, so everyone loses. The only way to curb your own irritable behaviour is to give it a time limit. Five minutes – no more. It is the only way. When it comes from another source, make your excuses and disappear until the air clears. There is no point in arguing with anyone if they are feeling irritable, because you will be on the receiving end until their equilibrium is restored.

Visualisation: Sitting on a beach, sunbathing with a group of friends, the laughter suddenly turns sour as one of the party becomes irritable after having had too much sun. An offer to escort them back to the hotel is dismissed, and the irritability continues until the entire group is affected and everyone splits up. The whole day is spoilt because of one person.

Affirmation: If I am irritated in company, I will keep smiling until I can be alone. Then I will deal with it.

90

❧

Inspiration

*Genius is one per cent inspiration and
ninety-nine per cent perspiration.*

Thomas Alva Edison
1847–1931

I THINK THE QUOTATION OPPOSITE certainly describes gyrating rock stars!

Where does inspiration come from, and how can you tap the source? If you are projecting your mind away from your physical body, as one does when trying to solve a problem or become absorbed in creativity, then your mind energy is released to expand and touch the Universal Mind. That is the source. How you extract what you need from it depends entirely on your ability to listen to the audible silence. There is no wasted space in the universe. From the beginning of time it has held the secrets of the cosmos, and, if you are patient, you will receive guidance. It is a tragedy that the world in which we live today values noise above the sanctuary of silence, for it is only there that you will find the key to inspiration.

If you are the kind of person who inspires others, remember always from whence *your* inspiration came, and be humble enough to acknowledge that you have only been given that same knowledge in order to pass it on for the good of others and not simply to impress or bolster your ego. In meditation I am always being reminded by my spiritual mentors that we are constantly being vetted and that ego has no value in the universe.

Visualisation: Tired and dispirited, you sit looking at a blank page. The dreaded writer's block has taken hold of you, and where inspiration previously allowed your artistic temperament to soar, now there is only a black void. Panic takes hold and depression sets in. Then you remember the mind energy; if it caves in it causes depression; if it expands it can touch the cosmos and the Universal Mind.

Sitting with eyes closed, you visualise the halo of mind energy being lifted from your brain and expanding ever outwards. You see it touching the light, and within seconds inspirational thoughts begin to flow. You open your eyes and begin to write. Page after page is filled with words that have inspired you and will inspire others.

Affirmation: Inspirational thought is a gift I must never abuse.

91

❧

Judgement

What judgement shall I dread, doing no wrong?

WILLIAM SHAKESPEARE
1564–1616

I DO NOT THINK that it is wise to judge others, because the full facts are rarely available. *'O what a tangled web we weave, When first we practise to deceive!'* This quotation by Sir Walter Scott is particularly relevant when the facts become embellished with exaggeration and fantasy. The simple explanation is that everyone's perception of the facts differs according to their emotional involvement. Trying to get to the truth of the matter is like walking through a minefield, and you could be blown away.

It is far better to listen and just be a friend than it is to judge.

Visualisation: You are listening to an argument between two friends. Accusations, like verbal missiles, are being hurled around and the atmosphere is charged with danger as they confront each other physically. Shouting above the noise, you ask them to stop. They both in turn ask you to see their point of view and beg you to side with them against the other. Although you can see both points of view, you are also aware that your views could fuel the fire even further, so you leave, knowing full well that any intervention would make things worse. At a later date you could sympathise with them both, but not now.

Affirmation: Judge not – lest ye be judged.

92

❧

Kindness

Tell them that, to ease them of their griefs,
Their fears of hostile strokes, their aches, losses,
Their pangs of love, with other incident throes
That nature's fragile vessel doth sustain
In life's uncertain voyage, I will some kindness do them.

WILLIAM SHAKESPEARE
1564–1616

T O BE KIND TO OTHERS costs nothing, and yet in the course of a day so many unkind words and gestures are exchanged wherever there are groups of people together that one wonders how the waves of positive energy around us and within us can be maintained. I do not believe those who maintain they are innocent of this human failing, for no matter how small the crime, unkindness is so common that it has become difficult to avoid falling into this particular pit. We should think before we act or speak, then perhaps we can replace the intended action or words with a little kindness. Try spreading it around wherever you may be. It could catch on, and completely change the atmosphere where you work, rest or play.

Visualisation: Shopping at your local supermarket, you notice a group of teenagers shouting unkind remarks to an elderly couple who, due to poor eyesight, are having problems reading labels and the price of the goods on the shelf. You feel embarrassed by the youths' behaviour but are hesitant to help the old couple as you are afraid that those same remarks will be directed at you. Then your kind nature overcomes your fear and you ask if they would like your help. Humiliated, they tell you they were about to leave. With a few kind words you persuade them to stay and you help them locate the items on their shopping list.

As you leave the store, one of the gang approaches you and you try to back away. 'Don't go,' he says. 'You have made me feel so ashamed. I just wanted to tell you that I am going to change.'

Affirmation: Kindness, like happiness, is catching.

93

Knowledge

Knowledge itself is power

<small>FRANCIS BACON</small>
1561–1626

THROUGHOUT MY LIFE I have never stopped seeking knowledge. When I am asked about my gifts, I always explain that being psychic is a sense of knowing. It does bring with it a kind of power, but one should not practise it without spirituality and an enormous sense of responsibility.

However, knowledge comes in many guises and that, I believe, is most exciting; you can be totally ignorant one minute, enlightened the next. It also comes in small packages, enabling us to absorb the subject matter in its entirety or learn only what we need for the moment. We choose what we learn; we have freedom of choice over what we know.

Through my mediumistic abilities I have had thousands of conversations with people who, when their minds had left their deceased bodies, found themselves being questioned about how much they had learned.

In meditation I have also been aware of the importance of seeking knowledge. It is apparently the key to the mysteries of the universe which, in our ignorance, continually confound us. There is so much to learn, and so little time. Don't waste it!

Visualisation: **While day-dreaming one day, you suddenly find yourself spinning out of your body towards an unseen destination. Totally relaxed, you give yourself up to the moment. Time is of no importance, and when you finally arrive at the end of your journey you are surprised to be asked by a Being of Light, 'What have you learned?' Having wasted most of your opportunities, you have no answer. You hear the voice again, only this time you are told to return and seek knowledge, for without it there can be no progress – not only on Earth but in any dimension.**

Affirmation: Without knowledge there is no progress. Without progress I can only stand still.

94

❧

Laughter

I made hay while the sun shone.
My work sold.
Now, if the harvest is over
And the world cold,
Give me the bonus of laughter
As I lose hold.

SIR JOHN BETJEMAN
1906–1984

LAUGHTER IS THE CATALYST for all healing. It releases the tensions from mind and body, allowing the free flow of energy which, in turn, stimulates every organ throughout the system. This increases the circulation of blood and thus revitalises the cells.

There are some who have inherited a mournful nature and who therefore find it very difficult to laugh. It is these people who repeatedly suffer minor afflictions, skin complaints in particular. The irritation that occurs whenever they hear others laugh manifests on the skin. I have cured thousands of people of all kinds of skin disorders by teaching them how to laugh at themselves.

Human beings are unbelievably (and usually unknowingly) funny. It is from ourselves that comedians draw all of their material, and that is where we have to start. No one is too rich or too famous to avoid the pitfalls that occur in our lives. The only way to save face – and health – is to laugh at our own stupidity and try not to repeat the gaffes.

Visualisation: **You are nervous as you meet your in-laws for the first time. A lovely meal has been prepared in your honour but, just as you sit down at the table, you accidentally knock some cutlery to the floor. Bending to pick it up, you drag the tablecloth with you and the beautifully prepared table is in chaos. When order has been restored and apologies made, you turn to your host and hostess and say, 'You didn't know that I was a born comedian did you?' Laughter resounds around the room as your host says, 'You fit in quite well, we're all crazy too.' The day has been saved, but if you had become upset and embarrassed everyone would have been miserable.**

Affirmation: Seeing the funny side of life keeps me happy and healthy.

95
❧

Laziness

*To the University of Oxford I acknowledge no
obligation; and she will as cheerfully renounce me for
a son, as I am willing to disclaim her for a mother. I
spent fourteen months at Magdalen College: they
proved the fourteen months the most idle and
unprofitable of my whole life.*

EDWARD GIBBON
1737–1794

S O MANY OPPORTUNITIES, so little time – and yet the young cast them aside without a second thought. There is no excuse for laziness. Even those who suffer from some disability often try harder than the healthy individuals who have been given a head start.

Depression can lead to laziness, for once the mind energy has become depressed and puts pressure on the brain, messages cease getting through to the body. If this is the problem, then think of one positive thing in your life and hold the image for as long as possible. This will eventually release the mind energy. Even joblessness doesn't need to result in laziness. The time (our most precious commodity) which the jobless now have in abundance can be used to learn a new trade or improve an existing one.

Lack of interest and boredom can also be turned around by focusing on the positive, and you get on with your life again. If you don't, failure will become a permanent word in your mental dictionary.

Visualisation: **Having rolled out of bed, you are busy trying to find a clean cup in which to make your first drink of the day, but everything is dirty. Looking around the kitchen in disgust, you wonder how you could have sunk to such a level. Wherever you look in your home it is untidy and dirty. With no job and no self-respect, you have idled away the hours, days and months in a stupor of boredom. Realising that things have gone too far, you spend the whole of the following week cleaning up. You also clean yourself up, so you set about washing and ironing all your clothes and having a haircut. When you have finished you are tired but infinitely happier.**

The following week a friend visits you, and as you invite them into your home a glow of self-respect warms your heart. Having returned to the land of the living you vow never to look back, because you know, with your new positive outlook, that there is something out there for you and you are going to find it.

Affirmation: Never look back. There is so much to do and so little time.

96

❦

Leisure

Increased means and increased leisure
are the two civilizers of man.

BENJAMIN DISRAELI
1804–1881

THE FASTER THE PACE OF LIFE BECOMES, the more leisure time you need. Your body clock contains only so much time, so it is absolutely essential to ensure that you do not run out of it and become ill. Do not make excuses for not taking time off for leisure; the regrets you have later in life will be all the more poignant if you destroy yourself through lack of quality time.

Visualisation: You are sailing around the world. Each day of the voyage reveals a part of your character you had not been in tune with for a long time. Indeed, as time goes by you realise that they are the best parts. You wish you had your life over again, so that these traits could have given pleasure rather than despair to those loved ones whom you had ignored so often. It is too late for regrets, but not too late to change. You have the rest of your life ahead of you.

Affirmation: Leisure is a pleasure I must not ignore.

97

❧

Lethargy

*This apoplexy is, as I take it, a kind of lethargy,
an't please your lordship; a kind of sleeping in the blood,
a whoreson tingling.*

WILLIAM SHAKESPEARE
1564–1616

AT SOME TIME OR ANOTHER, human beings experience lethargy. When it strikes, it feels as though a vacuum cleaner has sucked every ounce of energy from your body. Before taking any steps toward self-healing in any form, do have a medical check-up. When you have done that and, hopefully, been given a clean bill of health, take a good look at your life in general. The first thing you should check is nutrition. Are you eating sensibly? Bad eating habits mean that you may be deficient in vitamins and minerals. This is a common reason for feeling lethargic. Are you getting enough sleep? Are you working so hard that you can't relax even when you have time off? Or are you having a difficult relationship with someone? Whatever the cause you must sort it out, because lethargy is a great time waster and a strain on your health.

Visualisation: You have been feeling lethargic for some time and decide to analyse just what is going on in your life that has made you feel so low. Having had a medical check a few weeks ago and been given the all-clear, you know that the problem is not physical. You have cut out the junk food and relaxed a little. But sleeplessness is still bothering you because, as soon as your head hits the pillow, images of the difficulties you are encountering at work invade your mind. You confide in a friend, who suggests that you write down the good things that have happened that day and then the bad. Looking at the length of each column you find that, most nights, the positive column is much longer than the negative and you realise, for the first time, that you really don't have that much to worry about. You begin to sleep well and your energy levels rise. The lethargy disappears.

Affirmation: When I feel lethargic I will check out every aspect of my life.

98

❧

Love

*She bore about with her, she could not help
knowing it, the torch of her beauty; she carried it erect
into any room that she entered; and after all, veil it as she
might, and shrink from the monotony of bearing that it
imposed on her, her beauty was apparent. She had
been admired. She had been loved.*

VIRGINIA WOOLF
1882–1941

WHEN LOVE TOUCHES A HUMAN SOUL, it changes it for ever. The eyes, which are the windows of the soul, take on a brilliance that is not of this world, for pure love comes from a source which we can only feel. We can draw from this incredible energy because like attracts like. If *you* have a special *unselfish* love for someone, then this will strengthen and grow; if this love is not reciprocated, however, then your spirituality will help you to let go.

Do not make the error of mistaking lust for love. It is a common mistake and can lead to a disastrous relationship. You may be lucky and have both; when this happens, lust inevitably gives way and the stronger emotion of love takes over. Then, and only then, will you know contentment and peace, and feel the radiance from within.

Every living thing on this earth needs love. It is soul food, and without it we wither and die. Animals, in particular, give unselfish love.

Visualisation: Placing your hands on the shoulders of a friend who is in pain, you ask for help from the source of healing. Within seconds, you are both engulfed in a sensation hitherto unknown. It is a love so pure it defies description. Time does not exist as you give yourselves up to the experience. Later, when your friend's pain has disappeared, you can only wonder and thank God for the gift of healing.

Affirmation: To give love is to receive.

99

❧

Magic

When I came back from Lyonnesse
With magic in my eyes,
All marked with mute surmise
My radiance rare and fathomless,
When I came back from Lyonnesse
With magic in my eyes!

THOMAS HARDY
1840 – 1928

IF YOU HAVE TURNED TO THIS PAGE, then you are probably looking for a little bit of magic to brighten up your life. But why look for it? Why not conjure up a bit of magic for yourself? Waiting for someone else to do it for you could take a lifetime. All you need to do is to paint a picture with your mind, enhance and strengthen it daily, and you will soon be living with magic. Your imagery can take you into the realms of fact or fantasy. When you are adept at this you will be able to pull the picture through to this dimension because you are working with mind energy – the same energy that sends messages to the brain and body whilst we are alive and continues to exist when we leave this dimension. The mind is everlasting.

Visualisation: **Find a comfortable chair, and when you feel relaxed, close your eyes and start painting with your mental brush. A few brush strokes at a time is all that is needed to bring magic into your life. If you want something badly enough, then visualise the same picture every day. But if you only want a quick injection of fantasy, then dream on – give your imagination free rein. The inspiration you will receive from your pictures will also strengthen your perception, and this alone can turn failure into a success story. We all need magic, and we need it now!**

Affirmation: Magic will become part of my life from now on.

100

❧

Malice

With malice toward none; with charity for all; with firmness in the right, as God gives us to see the right, let us strive on to finish the work we are in: to bind up the nation's wounds; to care for him who shall have borne the battle, and for his widow and his orphan, to do all which may achieve and cherish a just and lasting peace among ourselves, and with all nations.

ABRAHAM LINCOLN
1809–1865

To FEEL MALICE toward any living thing is eventually to hate yourself for the thoughts that invade your mind. It is self-destructive. Practise the following visualisation as often as possible if you find yourself thinking malicious thoughts.

Visualisation: **You are being malicious towards someone, and feeling wonderful as you get rid of the darkness within you. Unfortunately, the negative vibes have attracted like energies which, strengthened, return. Within minutes your mind and body begin to feel the first pangs of total fatigue. Battered, and too tired to carry on, you try to revive yourself but the waves of negative energy continue to reverberate through your mind and body. In your desperation to escape from the nightmare you pray for help, and for the first time in your life you experience the gift of peace.**

Have the humility to ask for help and it will be given.

Affirmation: In future I will trust in Universal Law; I will refrain from being judge and jury.

101

Materialism

The black and merciless things
that are behind the great possessions.

HENRY JAMES
1843–1916

IF YOU HAVE A MATERIALISTIC NATURE, you could miss out on so many beautiful experiences that cost nothing. The simple life could give you far more, in peace and harmony, than any material possessions. It would be worth your while to check out how many things you could replace by changing and, having experimented, save yourself a lot of hard work, heartache, and money. Moderation in all things could change your life for ever and, without the stress, you could live longer.

Visualisation: Walking through a shopping arcade you are tempted, yet again, to overspend. You don't really need the articles that catch your eye but feel you must own them. Then your partner reminds you how many extra hours a week you are having to work to acquire these objects of desire, and suggests instead that you leave the arcade and stroll through the local park. You can see the reasoning behind the suggestion and you agree. Having admired the summer flowers, fed the ducks on the pond and soaked up the sunshine, you are thankful to have been given the chance to see that you have a problem and, by example, have been shown a healthier and less expensive alternative.

Affirmation: Inanimate objects cannot take the place of vibrant living things.

102

Meditation

Alas! I have nor hope nor health,
Nor peace within nor calm around,
Nor that content surpassing wealth
The sage in meditation found,
And walked with inward glory crowned.

PERCY BYSSHE SHELLEY
1792–1822

I CANNOT IMAGINE A LIFE without meditation, and look forward with eager anticipation to my allotted hour every day. After years of practice I have no need to go through the preliminaries – I simply close my eyes and leave this dimension behind. I have found that this has been a great bonus to me in my work as a medium.

Whilst meditating, the mind energy expands and links up to the cosmos. This way we can connect with the Universal Mind from whence we all receive inspiration. It also takes the pressure off the brain and body, allowing the energy to flow freely through the meridian lines (which are also used in acupuncture).

If you would like to try meditation in its simplest form, just sit down in a comfortable chair, close your eyes, and day-dream. Practise every day and you will soon be able to lose yourself in images that you have created with your mind. Creative imagination is the key to a less stressful life and a healthier lifestyle.

For those of you who would like to use meditation for self-healing, call up a picture in your mind of when you were fit and healthy. Hold that image for as long as possible and repeat the exercise twice a day. The message will reach every part of your body and your own chemistry will do the rest.

Visualisation: **Sit in a comfortable chair and close your eyes. In the distance you can see a bright white light; direct your thoughts toward the light and, as you do so, you will find yourself approaching it at great speed. When you reach the source your whole body will glow with its healing properties. Bask in it for a while and then think yourself back into the chair. When you are ready, open your eyes.**

Affirmation: I will meditate every day to keep stress at bay.

103

❧

Mediums

Where blind and naked Ignorance
Delivers brawling judgements, unashamed,
On all things all day long.

ALFRED, LORD TENNYSON
1809–1892

MEDIUMS HAVE EXPANDED mind energies that link in with minds in other dimensions, receiving and passing on messages from minds that have departed this Earth to friends and relatives who may be sitting with them. It takes years of practice to be gifted in this direction and it carries enormous responsibilities. Young mediums are often too eager to show their skills, not thinking about the consequences. Messages have to be translated so that they can be given to the recipient with the best possible taste and compassion. Like any other talent, one learns from mistakes, which is why this particular gift should be supervised for many years before anyone can call themselves a professional medium.

Mediums like myself inherit the gift, and grow up with a knowledge that is beyond all understanding to others. Whatever prejudice might sometimes exist against mediums – and most of it comes from ignorance – a born medium, like a born musician, has to live with their genetic inheritance. We must give of our time and compassion throughout our lives. It is not an easy life but a career that demands principles, discretion, and a high degree of responsibility; the end result should be loving and peaceful.

I have met many talented mediums who have deceived themselves into thinking that they are always right, and have consequently been drawn into a web of deceit from which they are unable to escape for fear of losing face. No medium is infallible. That is why, if you visit a medium, you should keep the messages you receive and use logic in applying any suggestions that have been made from a person who is no longer with you.

I have not given a visualisation for this word – if you think you are mediumistic, seek advice from a well-respected medium, and go from there.

Affirmation: Gifted mediums should be treated with the respect they deserve. They are not fortune-tellers.

104

❧

Memories

I've a grand memory for forgetting, David.

ROBERT LOUIS STEVENSON
1850–1894

I CANNOT IMAGINE A LIFE without memories. Beautiful, happy memories enhance our lives, and we can learn from the bad ones. Our higher minds usually protect us from the extreme negative effects of the bad memories but strengthen the life-giving properties of the positive.

For elderly people, happy memories are essential for health, and recalling them should not be discouraged. But no matter what age you may be, do try to store a mass of memories for the future. They could be your life-line when you need it most.

Visualisation: **If you are having a bad day, sit down and recall the happy memories that you have stored away in your mind. Hold the images so that they become stronger, and next time you need them they will be bolder and you will be able to fill in the gaps that were there the first time. Hold that dream.**

Affirmation: I will make a happy memory every day to ensure a bright future.

105

❧

Mind

Idleness is only the refuge of weak minds.

EARL OF CHESTERFIELD
1694–1773

M Y CLAIRVOYANT VISION and subsequent study of a bright white light around the head, which I called mind energy, encouraged me to write the *Mind* books that became bestsellers. If you would like to find the secret of mind energy, I suggest that you read the books *Mind to Mind, Mind Magic* and *Mind Waves*. They will set you on a journey that will not only open your mind but give you a direction that could change your life.

Like a computer, the mind is the power that drives the brain, and the more positive you are the more powerful you become. Negativity weakens the mind, body and spirit, and though it would be hard to banish negative thought altogether, never indulge in it for more than five minutes at a time.

Visualisation: You feel as though you are carrying the burdens of the world on your shoulders. Your body aches, your head aches, and you feel as though you have lead weights around your ankles. You decide that life could not get any worse.

Your partner suggests that you spend the little money you have on a weekend break in the country. As you walk together through the woods, you become aware of bright shafts of light penetrating the canopy of the great old oak and beech trees, the leaves shining with tinges of burnished gold. You look around and find that the autumnal shades are only a small part of a great mass of colour. The scene is breathtakingly beautiful, and as you feel the burdens you have carried for so long lift, you experience a lightness of heart that you had forgotten. Your partner smiles and says, 'The beauty of nature is the greatest healer of all. You simply haven't given yourself time to appreciate it.'

You make a pledge to yourself that no matter what problems may occur in the future, you are going to take time out, at regular intervals, to feel the healing essences of nature.

Affirmation: Positivity renews. Negativity destroys.

106

❧

Miracles

*By the time a man gets well into the seventies
his continued existence is a mere miracle.*

ROBERT LOUIS STEVENSON
1850–1894

MIRACLES DO HAPPEN. I have been privileged to have played some part in many hundreds of cases where a miracle has taken place; people who had been given a life sentence, and then reprieved; families that have been torn apart with quarrels, reunited through survival evidence; friends who have become bitter enemies, also reunited through clairvoyance and counselling; people who were in great pain with various illnesses and who had their health restored through healing. I could go on at length. Rest assured, miracles do happen, and in all the healing practices – whatever they may be – there are people whose caring is enough to give a bit of *oomph* to the process. If you can also do your bit, then your particular miracle could be nearer than you think.

Visualisation: Despite suffering an incurable spinal pain, you have decided to visit a spiritual guru who lives in a cave way up in the mountains. Before you made this journey you were warned that he might not speak to you but that you would come away with a gift. When you arrive at the entrance to the cave a soft voice bids you enter. When you meet this man you are mesmerised by the light in his eyes, you feel as though you are levitating, and you lose track of time.

With no knowledge of how you got there, you now find yourself standing on a ledge below the cave. You start to make your way back down the mountain when a voice from behind says, 'Having had the courage to make the journey, you have taken the first steps to enlightenment.'

Days later, you are astounded by the fact that your spinal pain is no longer there. You have experienced a miracle, but you also know that without those first painful steps, the miracle would never have happened.

Affirmation: I have to take the first step before I can expect a miracle.

107

❧

Mysticism

*I have often admired the mystical way of Pythagoras,
and the secret magic of numbers.*

Sir Thomas Browne
1605–1682

IT WOULD BE A BORING old world without mysticism. Apart from anything else, unbelievers would have to find some other target for their vehement prejudice. But there is nothing outwardly quite as sensational as the occult, so they would probably be bored to tears. Meanwhile, the lives of the believers would seem futile without the little bit of magic they know is readily available for the asking. So we simply cannot do without it.

Some mysticism can appear to be fantasy, but mystics themselves know that appearances can be deceptive, for they interact all the time with other dimensions and know the reality of them. Let's do a bit of dreaming.

Visualisation: You have been invited into the inner sanctum of a mystic's home. Everything appears to be normal, but within minutes you are enveloped in swirls of multi-coloured mists. The mystic speaks. 'If you could only choose one colour, which would it be?'

'I think they are all beautiful,' you reply. But as you look at the misty colours, you notice that the swirl that is most prominent is orange. 'I choose orange,' you say. The mystic smiles and leaves the room indicating that it is time for you to go. Angry, you say, 'But I was expecting something wonderful to happen.'

'It has,' replied the mystic, 'you have just learned a most important lesson. Never have expectations of others, for you will only be disappointed. Only have expectations of yourself, those you can make happen.'

Later, you are stopped by a man in the street. 'I have been asked to give you this,' he says, handing you a book. 'I was meditating,' he explains, 'and I received a message to take this book into the street and give it to a man with an orange cloak.'

Puzzled, you say, 'But I have no orange cloak.'

'You do in your energy field,' he replies.

On arriving home you open the book. It is empty, except for the title, 'EXPECTATIONS OF SELF WHICH I HAVE ATTAINED', and below, in small print, *'with a touch of magic'*. You know in an instant that *you* must write that book.

Affirmation: I will never have expectations of others, only of myself.

108

❧

Nightmares

History is a nightmare
from which I am trying to awake.

JAMES JOYCE
1882–1941

WHEN I HAVE BEEN HEALING, I have often been astounded at the incredible wisdom of some of my clients. This has been brought about by living the life that they have been given, and by dealing with nightmare situations as they came along. No one is exempt from them. Nightmares do occur, and you have to deal with them. Courage that has lain dormant for years will come to your aid, and you will be able to fight the demons and win. Remember, light attracts light, and if you do not allow yourself to sink to the depths of your tormentors, you will be all right.

The other kind of nightmare, the one you experience whilst sleeping, comes from a troubled mind. If you take time to think through your life and sort out the problems, your nightmares will gradually fade away.

Visualisation: You are afraid to retire every night because you are tormented by ghastly nightmares, and your health is suffering because of the interrupted sleep patterns. Unable to work, you are in danger of losing your job. You decide to visit a close friend. When you have finished confiding in him, he insists that you make two columns on a piece of paper. Under the headings 'Things I Love' and 'Things I Hate', he asks you to start writing. It is not long before it becomes painfully obvious that the Hate column is never-ending, and that this particular negative emotion is crippling your mind. Awareness compels you to act, and you go through the list eliminating the thoughts one-by-one until the nightmares disappear.

This exercise is really worthwhile – it really does work!

Affirmation: I will not allow my life to become a living nightmare.

109

❧

Noise

How many a father have I seen
A sober man, among his boys,
Whose youth was full of foolish noise.

ALFRED, LORD TENNYSON
1809–1892

THE WORLD IS SO FULL of noise that we are becoming incapable of listening to our innermost thoughts, those messages that come from the part of the mind that touches the source of all inspiration.

Unless one practises meditation it is impossible to listen to the audible silence that surrounds us, and through which we can learn to communicate without speech. The knowledge is there for the asking, but the noise factor has to be eliminated for at least an hour a day, every day, before we can absorb the vibrations of telepathic conversation.

Noise is crippling the natural waves of communication. It must be eliminated whenever possible to maintain the health of our mind, body and spirit.

Visualisation: **Your radio and television have been on all day, and you find that the non-stop conversation and music has given you a headache. You turn everything off, but peace evades you because your neighbour has his television on full blast. Hiding your head under a pillow you understand, for the first time, the damage you are doing to your health, and you also realise that you never give yourself time to think, that you have allowed other people's thoughts and ideas to take over your mind.**

The following day, you buy yourself a pad and pen, and you vow that you will have two hours silence every day so that you can listen and write down your own thoughts. You will take back your life, tuning into your own inspiration.

Affirmation: I need peace. I want my life back.

110

❧

Opportunism

The Devil watches all opportunities.

WILLIAM CONGREVE
1670–1729

OPPORTUNISTS HAVE NO PRINCIPLES, and prey on others when they are at their lowest ebb. They go to great lengths to create a sympathetic rapport with their victims and then they strike and leave, taking everything with them – money, homes, businesses, but most of all their victims' health. Or worse, they stay and squirrel everything away whilst giving the impression that they are only there to help. Most of them have charm and will go to great lengths to be popular. But their addiction also means that they frequently have to move on.

If you know someone like this, be careful. Seek out their old acquaintances and ask for their opinion. Do not ask their family, because in many cases they will be completely unaware of the addiction. If they are aware of it, as many will be after a while, you may find that they are loathe to say anything for fear of being ostracised from a larger circle of friends. Lack of courage in these instances goes a long way in letting the perpetrator off the hook and, as always, the innocent continue to suffer.

You may be working and living with someone like this. If so, do not sign *anything* until you have sought the advice of a reputable solicitor. Keep your eyes open at all times and do not let your heart rule your head.

Visualisation: You have recently lost your husband, and an apparently sympathetic person walks into your life. He tells you that you only have to ask if you need financial help. He gives the impression that he has been a financial director, which builds your confidence in him. He asks about the business you and your husband owned and offers to help out with the accounts. In other words, he is fantastic. It seems that he can cure your loneliness and anything else that may be causing unhappiness. He is your knight in shining armour.

Flattered, you take it all in, and after a few months a new marriage is on the cards. But one morning you realise that you have lost control of your life and your finances and it looks highly likely you will eventually lose everything.

You have had a lucky escape.

Affirmation: Don't trust the smiling stranger at the door.

111

❧

Opportunities

*A wise man will make more opportunities
than he finds.*

FRANCIS BACON
1561–1626

IF YOU HAVE THE OPPORTUNITY to enhance your life, take it. If you don't, make sure you don't waste energy regretting a lost opportunity later. This is negative. You should just put it down to experience and look forward to grabbing the next one that comes along with both hands. Better still, *make* them happen.

The majority of opportunities are lost through laziness, fear, or lack of self-confidence. Try to eradicate these obstacles from your life and you will be on a winning streak.

Visualisation: You have been offered a post abroad. The dream that you have seen so often in your imagination has materialised. As the time for you to move gets closer, your self-confidence takes a dive and the fears begin. Thoughts of failure seep into your mind. Looking around your comfortable home, you realise that the safety net will be broken. You are taking chances. Your friends and family will not be around to comfort you.

Then the excitement of a new beginning takes over, as does the knowledge that you want to be a whole human being, able to take life as it comes, and later, to have incredible memories. You opt for the new job. In doing so you have jumped your first hurdle.

Affirmation: I can rise above the fears. I will not fail.

112
❧

Peace

Over all the mountain tops is peace.

JOHANN WOLFGANG VON GOETHE
1749–1832

WHAT IS PEACE? It is a sensation so elusive that it could take a lifetime to find. The path to it, strewn with our own unique inadequacies, is a maze through which we stumble and fall; yet in the seeking, an awareness of our own self-worth will emerge and we will learn that the peace that we seek is within us and not in a fantasy that we have conjured up with our minds. The journey will be hard but the rewards are great, for without peace we have nothing.

Visualisation: Your lifestyle has become stressful, and you know that your mind and body need a break from the relentless day-to-day effort that your job demands. Surrounded by holiday brochures, every picture looks enticing, but as the minutes tick by you find that even this decision is causing unnecessary hassle. In a flash of inspiration you make the final choice. You will stay within the confines of your home, sleep, read, listen to music, eat and exercise without any regime or interference from outside influences. It offers greater freedom by far than catching planes, trains, boats and having to suffer other people's idiosyncrasies. At last you have become aware of the greatest gift of all. Peace within.

Affirmation: If changes are necessary to find the peace within, I will make them.

113

❦

Pessimism

*The optimist proclaims that we live in the best
of all possible worlds and the pessimist fears
this is true.*

JAMES BRANCH CABELL
1879–1958

PESSIMISM IS THE WORST KIND of negativity, because it does not allow any positive thought to intrude into the mind of this grey twilight world. The glass is always half empty, never half full. The pessimist sees the optimist as an enemy who is ever hopeful of dragging their dark thoughts through to the light. It is quite possible that this problem is inherited, but most likely it is activated by a series of disasters until the person feels victimised. Either way, it has to be dealt with if it is not going to ruin the life of the pessimist. When the mind energy caves in and presses on the brain – as it does with all negative thought – blockages in the energy system will stop all the major organs vibrating and the health deteriorates. If you feel that you cannot be happy and have nothing to live for, then stir yourself and *make* something happen, because nobody else will. Misery is the first thing that turns other people away.

Visualisation: All your life you have been a pessimist. One day you meet a tramp. He has rags on his back and no shoes, but as you walk by he smiles. You turn back and ask him what he has to smile about. 'I was smiling at your miserable face,' he says. 'And you with a nice suit and good shoes, you should be happy.' Feeling ashamed, you hand him enough money to buy some shoes.

Days later, you see the tramp again. This time he has shoes on his feet. 'So you bought the shoes, then?' you remark.

'Yes,' he replies, 'and I was so happy with them that the owner of the shop thought I deserved a few clothes to go with them. Look in here.' He points to a bag by his side. You look in the bag and find that it is full of new clothes. 'You see, if you spread a little sunshine into other people's lives you will be rewarded.' He pauses as if in thought. 'Perhaps *your* life will change now.' He turns away, laughing to himself.

Walking home, you find that you have a lightness of step that you haven't experienced for a long time, and the pessimism you have felt for so long has suddenly lifted. Colours also seem to have taken on a brighter hue, and you know that you will not be returning to the grey world in which you have been living for so long.

Affirmation: My world must be full of colour.

114

❦

Pettiness

*Why, man, he doth bestride the narrow world
like a Colossus; and we petty men
Walk under his huge legs, and peep about
To find ourselves dishonourable graves.
Men at some time are masters of their fates:
The fault, dear Brutus, is not in our stars,
But in ourselves, that we are underlings.*

WILLIAM SHAKESPEARE
1564–1616

PETTINESS IS UNNECESSARY and unkind. It is also a huge waste of time and talent, even boring when carried to extremes. It tends to bring out the worst in people and does not achieve positive results, for although you may think you have won the first round, it can turn on you and reveal the embarrassing weak traits in your character. Pettiness will give a truer picture of yourself than you could ever imagine.

Visualisation: **Your partner is behaving in an extremely petty manner, and the atmosphere in your home is cold and miserable. It is not the first time this has happened and you know that it will not be the last unless you do something about it, so you leave with a small overnight case to stay with a friend.**

Two days later you return to your home and you warn your partner that you will leave every time the pettiness returns, that you will not endure it any longer. Your warnings are taken to heart and the pettiness ends, but you know that if it ever returns you can walk away.

Affirmation: I can walk away rather than endure petty behaviour.

115

❧

Phenomena

Language was not powerful enough to describe the
infant phenomenon.

CHARLES DICKENS
1812–1870

PARANORMAL PHENOMENA in my own world are so common that I tend to overlook the small examples that are almost a weekly occurrence. I do, however, understand that it can be very difficult to come to terms with if you are not familiar with the paranormal. Incidents are initiated from other dimensions, to create and make an impression to achieve a goal. It could be in healing, in mediumship, or in meditation. Some spontaneous phenomena can happen to people who have no interest in the paranormal at all – these are the most exciting, because they make you think and, where hitherto you had been an unbeliever, you are now inclined to believe. The paranormal does exist, and maybe one day something special will happen to you.

Visualisation: Having been told by a friend that you are receiving healing for a sports injury, you gently mock her for her belief. 'Wait and see,' she replies. You are awoken that night by a feeling of warmth and tingling running through your body, and then you become aware that a small bright blue light is hovering above your head. It stays for a few minutes, then disappears. This is your first experience of the phenomenon of distant healing, and you know that you will never forget.

Affirmation: An open mind is the key to the secrets of the universe.

116

❧

Phobias

Because the road is rough and long,
Shall we despise the skylark's song?

ANNE BRONTË
1820–1849

PHOBIAS COME FROM a deep-rooted fear of life that impinges itself on a particular subject or object – they are the effect, not the cause. Rid yourself of the fear in your subconscious and you will find that the phobia will disappear. There are many clinics where you can seek help, or find a reliable hypnotist who can get to the root of the problem. Fear is your arch-enemy, you must find the cause, face it and learn from it, otherwise the phobias will increase and get completely out of hand.

Visualisation: Your phobic nature has caused so much unhappiness in your life that you decide to find a registered hypnotist. Although you fear the session, you make the effort to attend. He is able to help you with the phobia but also releases unhappy memories that have been hidden in your subconscious for years. Two months later you are cured, fear no longer plays a part in your everyday existence and you cannot remember a time when you have felt so happy and free. You now know that you can look forward to a future without phobias and the knowledge that fear can be expelled.

Affirmation: Abolish fear and the phobias will disappear.

117

❦

Positivity

Injustice, poverty, slavery, ignorance – these may be cured by reform or revolution. But men do not live only by fighting evils. They live by positive goals, individual and collective, a vast variety of them, seldom predictable, at times incompatible.

SIR ISAIAH BERLIN
1909–1997

A POSITIVE OUTLOOK ON LIFE is your health insurance for the future. Having studied mind energy for twenty-five years, I am even more convinced now than I was at the beginning that this energy is the key to universal knowledge and to our own potential. Where positivity is concerned, the thought is the deed.

Distant healing is an example of this. The mind energy reaches its destination and carries out the deed with the help of other entities. But the other entities would not become involved unless triggered by positive thought. You do not have to believe in the paranormal to test the efficiency of a positive approach to life. You will find that, with practice, it will turn your life around, failure will be replaced with success, and your whole being will glow with health.

Visualisation: Every time you are tempted to be negative, reverse your thoughts, and through your imagination visualise the success you will achieve by this simple switch. Turning negative to positive also reverses the energy so that instead of caving in and pressing on the brain and body it will expand, reaching out into the cosmos, enabling you to touch your source of inspiration.

Affirmation: Positive thought, success. Negative thought, failure.

118

❧

Possession

Farewell thou art too dear for my possessing . . .

WILLIAM SHAKESPEARE
1564–1616

MANY PEOPLE HAVE ASKED for my help because they have felt they were being possessed by an evil entity. Explaining that they themselves were actually attracting the negative energy was at times extremely difficult for them, but it is a fact. Energy attracts like to like, and if you are in a negative state yourself, then you will encourage like minds to attach themselves to you. Whatever the cause of your state of mind, you must erase the negativity or it will return and attack you mentally or physically – or both.

The same applies to mischievous people, who attract equally mischievous minds. This is especially apparent when there is poltergeist activity around children.

If you feel that you are being possessed in any way, analyse your own emotions and erase all negativity from your personality. Think only pleasant thoughts. I have proved time and again that these spirits have a low boredom threshold – if they cannot disturb you they will soon be on their way.

Visualisation: **Walking through your home you can feel unpleasant vibes which disturb you. Knowing that like attracts like you hastily rearrange your thoughts and say the Lord's Prayer. The change is immediate, and you feel a warm enveloping cloak of energy surround you. You feel peaceful and contented, and happier than you have felt for some time, and you vow never to allow negative thoughts to drag you so low again.**

Affirmation: My mind will always be full of light to keep the darkness out.

119

Possessiveness

Being your slave, what should I do but tend
Upon the hours and times of your desire?
I have no precious time at all to spend,
Nor services to do, till you require.
Nor dare I chide the world-without-end hour
Whilst I, my sovereign, watch the clock for you,
Nor think the bitterness of absence sour
When you have bid your servant once adieu;
Nor dare I question with my jealous thought
Where you may be, or your affairs suppose,
But like a sad slave, stay and think of nought
Save, where you are, how happy you make those.
So true a fool is love that in your will,
Though you do anything, he thinks no ill.

WILLIAM SHAKESPEARE
1564–1616

I THINK THE QUOTATION OPPOSITE says it all. Possessiveness is a misery for all concerned. Once drawn into this fatal web, it is very difficult to extract yourself from the deceiving but beautiful steel-like filaments that stifle all the life from the victim. It also leads to a slow death for the perpetrator, because they cannot relax their vigil. Partnerships, friendships and marriages cannot last if possessiveness is at the core of the relationship. It can only bring great unhappiness to those who are involved.

Visualisation: **You are possessive about your partner, but you realise that trying to keep tabs on another person all the time is making you ill. Someone suggests that you take a back seat for a while so that you can reclaim the exciting life you had before this relationship began. Although it makes sense, you confide in your friend that you think it will be impossible, as your possessiveness has taken over your life. 'Okay,' they remark, 'then I'll take you away with me for a couple of weeks.' Your bags are packed and you are shunted off to the nearest airport.**

Two weeks later you return home to find every room filled with flowers, and you know that trust and love has replaced the possessiveness that had so nearly destroyed you both.

Affirmation: Possessiveness kills love.

120

❧

Potential

Books are not absolutely dead things, but do contain a potency of life in them to be as active as that soul was whose progeny they are; nay they do preserve as in a vial the purest efficacy and extraction of that living intellect that bred them.

JOHN MILTON
1608–1674

THE FIRST PART OF THIS WORD is 'potent'. As the quotation states, it is the potency of life that enables one to reach one's potential. You have a winning formula when this is combined with a completely open mind. But when the mind is open you will be made aware that you are a vital part of the universe, but you have to give before you can receive. However, another gift will help you on the way, and that is compassion. If you are wholly aware, this emotion will play a great part in your life and the lives of others, and through it you will receive.

We are not islands; we are *part of the substance* that creates the vortices and waves of energy that sweep through the cosmos embracing and enfolding us, and our participation is on-going, through many lives. Supported in this immense, vast bed of energy, how can we *not* give of our best?

Visualisation: You are being held in a vast sea of energy, restless, undulating, suddenly riding the crest of a wave and then sinking into the depths. When you are riding the crest you feel as though you can challenge the world. While in the depths you feel unable to control the energies around you and are unable to think clearly. You are being shown what it is like when you have the potency of life to reach your potential, and what it feels like when you haven't. Remember this exercise and use it often – you will need it!

Affirmation: I will show compassion to those I meet on my way up, because I could meet them coming down.

121

❦

Public speaking

The life so short, the craft so long to learn.

HIPPOCRATES
5th Century BC

THERE IS AN ART to public speaking that can only be learned by going out there and doing it. There are, however, many things that you can do to ease the way. First, practise at home alone, then when you are more confident ask a relative or friend whom you can trust to listen to you. Do not have several people present, because too many ideas can spoil the whole thing and you will only become confused. Then try to give your speech from memory, as this makes for a more relaxed presentation. If your memory is not good or if you get nervous in public, type or write out notes on cards in large print that will be easy to follow, and staple it all together as far back into the left hand corner as you can for ease of turning.

Do not, if you can help it, drink alcohol before you speak, as this can lead to a total disaster. Instead, think outwards to an imaginary bright star. This will keep your mind active and, at the same time, remind yourself that you are the star turn. Good luck!

Visualisation: **You are at a dinner and it is time for you to go to the rostrum to make your speech. Your legs are shaking and you are finding it difficult to stand. Then you think of the star, and direct your mind toward the bright light. Immediately, you feel the weakness in your legs leaving, and you are able to stand. Feeling strong and confident, you go forward and make the best speech of your life. When you return to your table, your head still ringing from the applause, you know that you have buried the doubt that has kept you a prisoner for so long, and that, in future, your star will burn brighter.**

Affirmation: My star will shine ever brighter as I work towards my goals.

122

❧

Predictions

Mr Turnbull had predicted evil consequences . . . and was now doing the best in his power to bring about the verification of his own prophecies.

ANTHONY TROLLOPE
1815–1882

M Y STUDY OF THE MIND has proved that it is essential for everyone to build up images of what they want to achieve, and to hold that dream. Then, at a later date, it will materialise in this dimension. This way you are predicting your own future and *your* life is in *your* hands. You will have complete control and responsibility for self. Predictions from others take away that control and then you become dependent and that weakens the character.

Predictions can be extremely accurate, but they should be used only as a guideline and not as something to base one's life upon, especially if they are of the negative kind. Use your common sense if you want to see into the future, and make sure that you use the information only as a line to hold on to when things are bad, and not as a substitute for thinking for yourself.

Visualisation: You have no idea what you want to do with your life. Then you are asked by a friend to accompany them to meditation classes. Although the idea does not really appeal, you agree to go. In the meditation you find yourself standing in a field, with a backdrop of mountains to one side, water on the other, and behind you a flat landscape. You have to make a choice, and you choose to take the path towards the water. At this point the teacher brings you out of your trance.

After everyone else has been asked what they had perceived, it is your turn to share your experience. When you have finished, the teacher says, 'You made the right choice.' She explains that going towards the mountains would mean that you would have an uphill struggle to find your natural talent, and that by turning back and walking in the direction of the flat landscape your path would be easy but boring. By choosing the path toward the water, you were walking towards energy, movement and a chance to ride the waves to an exciting future.

'But I *still* don't know what I want to do,' you reply, rather tetchily. The teacher smiles. 'Don't you see? You are being told that you do have a future, and that says it all. You have talent, although at the moment it is hidden, and you have the capacity and courage to seek and find. What more could you want?'

Affirmation: My footsteps will take me into the unknown, for where else will I find the key to my destiny?

123

❧

Pride

'The whole of this unfortunate business,' said Dr Lyster, 'has been the result of PRIDE AND PREJUDICE.'

FANNY BURNEY
1752–1840

PRIDE CAN PREVENT YOU asking for help when you need it most. I have known couples in desperate need who were too proud to ask their children for help, yet their offspring would have jumped at the chance of helping their parents. Pride can mean that people lie to their loved ones and their friends and, in so doing, burden them with guilt when something happens later on. It is also true that pride goes before a fall, so if you need help, *ask for it.*

Pride is a curse when it prevents you saying a few kind words to someone you love. Don't be too proud to admit that you have been wrong. How dull you would be if you were perfect!

Visualisation: It is a very cold winter and, although you have coal for the fire, you haven't the strength to carry it from outside your isolated farmhouse to your fireside. You use the electric heaters, but storms are causing havoc with the main generators, so there are times when you have to do without any heat at all.

Every morning you watch as a neighbour passes by your cottage on his motorbike, and although you are tempted to ask for his help, your pride will not allow it. You quickly succumb to the flu, and when your friend visits, she weighs up the situation and is cross that you haven't asked for help. 'Your pride will kill you one day,' she says crossly. That evening, her husband and son come to visit and ask for your permission to carry out some work in your home. When you ask them what they are going to do, they say, 'Trust us.' Lying in bed, you can hear thumps and bangs and wonder what on earth is happening. When they have finished they invite you downstairs to sit by the fire. With shaking legs you walk down the stairs and into the sitting-room and, to your amazement, you find that they have built a steel chute through the wall from the coal bunker outside; all you have to do to reach your coal is open a door and let it tumble into a large container by the fireplace. Shocked and impressed, you mumble your thanks. When they have gone you realise that if you had hung on to your pride it would probably have killed you. Instead, an innovative idea has relieved you of the constant worry of keeping warm.

Incidentally, this is a true story.

Affirmation: People need to be needed. I will ask for help when I cannot cope.

124

❧

Principles

I am afraid he has not been in the inside of a church
for many years;
but he never passes a church without pulling off his hat.
This shews that he has good principles.

SAMUEL JOHNSON
1709–1784

Throughout life you will find that others will try to seduce you with promises of wealth. But in many cases, attaining it quickly or easily would mean that you have to forget your principles, and this would inevitably result in a downward trend in your life. Your health would be the first thing to be affected because subconsciously you would feel guilty, and guilt is an extremely negative emotion that harms the psyche. Illness would quickly follow, and then it would be downhill all the way. It simply is not worth it. If sticking to your principles means that you miss out on wealth, you won't have missed much, and the older you get the more you will realise the truth of this statement. It is much more important to build on the foundations of health and happiness. If material things come later they will give far more pleasure as you have earned the right to own them.

Visualisation: You have an appointment for a job that you know will take you out of the gloomy flat you live in with your partner. But during the interview it is made clear to you that you would have to forgo principles that you were taught by your parents and to which you yourself subscribe. For a few moments you are tempted. But then you see the image of your parents and you know that they and your partner would be disappointed in you if you acquired wealth in this way. You regretfully turn down the appointment and turn to leave. 'One moment,' the chairman says. 'If you would like the job, it is yours.' Bemused, you look questioningly at his smiling face. 'This appointment needs someone we can trust,' he says. 'To ensure that I got the right man for the job I had to test your principles.'

Affirmation: Stick to your principles and you will have your just rewards.

125

❦

Priorities

The heavens themselves, the planets, and this centre
Observe degree, priority and place,
Insisture, course, proportion, season, form,
Office, and custom, in all line of order.

TO HAVE ORDER IN YOUR LIFE, you must get your priorities right. It is usually quite easy to recognise the order in which they should be placed, but where emotions are involved, mistakes can be made which lead to misunderstandings and lost friendships. The urgency of some situations does not give you time to think, just act, and this is a good way to sort out the rest. Try the following exercise.

Visualisation: **Take a pen and paper and write down what you consider to be your priorities. When you have done that, act them out one by one in your mind. This will give you a good idea of the end result. It will also highlight the mistakes you might be making in your order of priorities. As you go through the list, you will find that the most urgent will produce the strongest reaction in you; these you must put at the top. Go on rearranging your list until you feel that you have got it right. Then you can act. Gradually your judgement will improve, and then you can dispense with the pen and paper.**

Affirmation: I will take time to get my priorities right.

126

※

Privacy

Private faces in public places
Are wiser and nicer
Than public faces in private places

W. H. AUDEN
1907–1973

I T IS ABSOLUTELY ESSENTIAL that everyone has some privacy in their lives. Our minds and bodies need regular rejuvenation, and this is not possible unless privacy is available, even if it is in small doses. If you are desperate, there is always one small room in every house where no one can follow! With effort it can afford you a small amount of time to collect your thoughts. This room can be your salvation, especially if you have a crowded home.

Alternatively, let it be known that you want half an hour to yourself when everyone else has gone to bed. This time could be spent in meditation or day-dreaming. Either way, you will be revitalising your mind and body.

Find a way to have your private moments, and you will never look back.

Visualisation: **Having tried and failed to gain some privacy, you awake one night with toothache. Getting out of bed, you make your way downstairs to take a painkiller. As you relax in the armchair, you realise that someone has shown you the way. You are alone, it is peaceful and you have the privacy you have longed for. At that moment you assure yourself that this quiet moment will be your secret and can happen again any night you choose.**

Affirmation: Where there is a will, there is a way.

127

❧

Quarrels

*Thrice blest (and more) are the couple whose ties are
unbroken and whose love, never strained by nasty
quarrels, will not slip until their dying day.*

HORACE
65–8 BC

I CANNOT IMAGINE that there is anyone who has not quarrelled at some time in their lives. We begin as soon as we are able to walk, snatching other children's toys and screaming when we cannot get our own way. However nice you are, as children or adults, when the nasties get at you, it is extremely difficult to avoid quarrels! To protect our health we have to cut down the negative impact that quarrels have on us by ignoring stupid and unimportant issues. Fatigue tends to make us more irritable, so when you feel tired turn the other cheek if you sense someone wants to quarrel with you. Save your energy for the important things in life, and especially save it for those who cannot fight for themselves.

If possible, make light of the situation when a quarrel is brewing, and try to see the funny side of life. When you think about it, the way people act most of the time is hilarious.

Visualisation: You can feel the heaviness of the atmosphere in your home and you know that trouble is brewing. Then you hear quarrelling in the children's bedroom. As you enter the room your two daughters stop shouting and look guiltily at each other. You ask them to stop quarrelling, and then you tell them to look in the mirror. One girl's face is red with anger and covered in blotches, the other girl's eyes are red and swollen where she has been crying. 'Just look at yourselves,' you say laughingly. 'Is quarrelling really that important? You look like a couple of clowns!' Putting your arms about them, you make them laugh at themselves and the atmosphere changes. You say, 'You know, I could feel the energy you were wasting from downstairs. It really isn't worth it, is it?' They nod in agreement. Later they had to admit that their anger had drained them as they were unable to concentrate on their homework.

People waste energy like this all the time. It is only when you are ill that you realise what a precious commodity it is.

Affirmation: I have time for intelligent conversation but I have no time for quarrels.

❧

128

Reincarnation

To every thing there is a season, and a time to every
purpose under the heaven:
A time to be born, and a time to die; a time to plant,
and a time to pluck up that which is planted;
A time to kill, and a time to heal; a time to break
down, and a time to build up;
A time to weep, and a time to laugh; a time to mourn,
and a time to dance;
A time to cast away stones, and a time to gather stones
together; a time to embrace, and a time to refrain from
embracing;
A time to get, and a time to lose; a time to keep, and a
time to cast away;
A time to rend, and a time to sew; a time to keep
silence, and a time to speak;
A time to love, and a time to hate; a time of war, and
a time of peace.

THE BIBLE, ECCLESIASTES

THERE IS ALSO A TIME to be reborn. Mankind's progression is dependent on a free passage back and forth from one dimension to another.

There has been abundant evidence of reincarnation from scientific and medical sources, and also from parents who have been astounded at the images of a past life conveyed by their children. Babies as young as eighteen months have, in their innocence, given the world faith in the concept of the everlasting mind. All of this information is conveniently forgotten by those who do not know better, but stories on the subject of reincarnation appear in books around the world and provide irrefutable evidence.

There were the twins who died in a car accident. Their mother gave birth to another set of twins and, when they were old enough, their personalities were exactly the same as their predecessors. They even chose the same toy cupboard and toys.

There was the case of the Indian boy who told his mother that he used to own a shop in another village. When investigators took him there, he recognised his children when they arrived outside the shop, and named them. He admonished his widow for changing everything around in the shop. He was also able to give details of his violent death.

There was a little girl in America born with a scar on her neck. When she was two years old, she told her mother that she remembered living in a different country and that someone had cut her throat. As she got older more details emerged, and when she was five a scientific investigator took her to the small village in India she had named. There she pointed out her previous mother's house, noting that the colour had been changed. She was also able to point out an old man who, she said, had cut her throat whilst she was in her pram. These facts were all found to be correct.

I have not given a visualisation for this word because reincarnation is based on knowledge. When we are ready to reincarnate, then we will know more.

Affirmation: The mind is everlasting. We never cease to exist.

129

❦

Rejection

The liberty of the individual must be thus far limited;
he must not make himself a nuisance to other people.

JOHN STUART MILL
1806–1873

REJECTION IS VERY DIFFICULT to deal with, especially when a loving relationship comes to an end. The pain for the person who is being subjected to this treatment is indescribable, and yet it would only be another kind of hell to force someone to stay. Like all the other traumas that occur during our lives, we simply have to deal with it.

You can experience another kind of rejection if you insist on pursuing someone when they have made it clear that your attentions are unwanted. No matter how you may perceive the situation, you must not invade another person's space without their permission. Therefore, although the treatment that is being meted out to you may seem severe and unwarranted, you must understand that negative thought attracts like thought, and this could cause you even more unnecessary pain. Look for the positive and put the negative behind you. You don't need it. Neither do you need someone who rejects you. Why put yourself in this position, when you are worth so much more?

Visualisation: **You are pursuing someone who has made it clear that they do not intend to return the affection you have for them. Your feelings for them are so intense that you ignore the vibes that you are getting, but your mind and body react violently to them, and you have to think again. Feeling tired and miserable, you decide to back off and get a life. Within days your energy returns and you leave behind 'what might have been' and think about 'what will be'. With positive imagery, you know that you can achieve your goals, and that happiness will follow.**

Negative situations can be turned around by one single thought.

Affirmation: I will deal with rejection, and get a life!

130

❧

Reputation

Indeed the Idols I have loved so long
Have done my credit in this World much wrong:
Have drown'd my Glory in a Shallow Cup
And sold my Reputation for a Song.

EDWARD FITZGERALD
1809–1883

IT IS ABSOLUTELY ESSENTIAL that you safeguard your reputation. No matter what status you may have in life, having a good reputation will bring you the respect of others, and this is very important. It will open doors that could otherwise remain closed. Opportunities will come your way because people trust you with their confidences. Above all, you will be known to have honour.

It is not easy to keep your reputation if someone is determined to undermine it. Jealousy abounds, and if you are seen to be fair-minded and compassionate there are those who will deliberately mark you down as weak-minded, so that they can wear your mantle. It would not fit them, however, and others would soon recognise a fake. It takes a special kind of person to acquire the mantle in the first place.

Keeping your reputation intact will make you feel good. This, in turn, will keep you happy and healthy.

At all costs avoid people with bad reputations.

Visualisation: You have been enjoying the company of a special circle of friends for some years, but then one of them introduces a person of bad repute into the circle. You know instinctively that this person spells trouble, but the others do not agree. To protect yourself and your reputation you leave your friends behind and move on. It is a very difficult decision, but you know it to be the right one.

Over the next two years, you see your old friends' lives disintegrating. One by one they choose the wrong paths because they have listened to the Judas in their midst. It turns out that the Judas had been so jealous of this close-knit circle of friends that he deliberately set out to destroy them. Your instincts were correct.

Affirmation: If something instinctively feels wrong, I shall keep away from it.

131

❦

Retirement

For solitude sometimes is best society,
And short retirement urges sweet return.

JOHN MILTON
1608–1674

RETIREMENT CAN BE either a very difficult time or the icing on the cake, depending on your circumstances. To remain healthy, though, you should keep busy. If you have been used to a disciplined career, keep a certain amount of that discipline in your retirement years, otherwise the 'shock factor' to the mind and body can cause problems. Allow your mind to change the blueprint for your life gradually. That way you will see a picture emerging that could delight and entertain you. Don't have a closed mind about your future. Go with the flow.

Boredom is the greatest and sometimes the most surprising element. After waiting years for the chance to relinquish your career and put your feet up, you may find that you are bored to death with ordinary, everyday existence. If this is a problem for you, then look around, make new friends and start a new hobby. Whatever you do, don't just sit at home and mope. If you are happy, then your health will benefit.

Visualisation: **You retired eighteen months ago, and are living alone. Bored with your own company, you decide to look at the entertainment provided by local societies. None of them appeal to you, until you notice a card advertising a beginner's class for bridge. It is something you have always wanted to learn but haven't had the time to study. You enrol, and meet a circle of people who quickly become your friends. Before long, you find yourself travelling to various parts of the country taking part in bridge matches, and you wonder how you had ever had the time to feel bored.**

There is something out there for everyone; you simply have to look for it. Retirement does not mean that you have to retire from life – it is the beginning of a New Life.

Affirmation: Life is for living.

132

❦

Runes

Not as their friend or child I speak!
But as on some far northern strand,
Thinking of his own Gods, a Greek
In pity and mournful awe might stand
Before some fallen Runic stone –
For both were faiths, and both are gone.

MATTHEW ARNOLD
1822–1888

THE RUNES ARE AN ANCIENT alphabetical script, usually inscribed on a set of stones. A rune caster will throw them and then read them. I have used runes for many years, especially if the forecast is for someone I know well. They enable me to bypass the physical and find the soul of that person. If you would like to know more about runes, there are many books on the subject – I particularly recommend *The Book of Runes* by Ralph Blum, obtainable from your local book shop.

Visualisation: In your dreams, you continually visit a strange land and find that you are surrounded by huge stones carved with an unknown script. The dream is so frequent that it invades your waking life. One day a friend invites you to visit a rune caster. As soon as you see the stones you recognise the script of your dreams. When it is time to leave, the rune caster turns to you and says, 'You recognised the stones, didn't you?' When you agree, and tell him about your dreams, he smiles, and says, 'Old haunts of this nature are difficult to relinquish. You had magic in your life then, and you will have it again, because *you* were a rune caster in a past life. We will meet again.'

Many years later you do meet again. Placing a hand on your arm he says, 'As a rune caster you are the best, because you never forget the basics you learned in your past life – that when you throw the runes for yourself you are consulting an Oracle which will show you a mirror image of self, and by recognising the self, you have the freedom of choice. You have wisdom far beyond your years, and you are using it wisely.'

Affirmation: I will be true to my own self.

133

❧

Sacrifices

The universe is so vast and so ageless that the
life of one man can only be justified by the measure of
his sacrifice.

PILOT OFFICER V. A. ROSEWARNE
1916–1940
Last letter to his mother, published in
The Times 18 June 1940

MAKING SACRIFICES is part and parcel of living. Parents continually make sacrifices for their children and, as the children grow up and the parents age, this is hopefully reciprocated. We need help at both ends of the age spectrum.

Love is the main reason for giving up something special to enrich another person's life. But not the only one. All people in caring professions give their energies and free time to help those in need. Strangers are blessed by their generosity of spirit and compassion.

If you are asked to make sacrifices to help someone, and there is no other way of dealing with the situation, then do it. You will never regret it, because whatever you give you will eventually receive.

Visualisation: Your partner has booked the holiday of a lifetime, but two weeks before your departure a dear friend falls ill. She has no family, and no friends that she wants near her at this particular time. You are the only person with whom she has a special relationship.

You do not want to upset your partner, but neither do you want to leave your friend, especially as she is quite old. What should you do? Arguments ensue, but you eventually make the decision to stay with your friend. However, ten days later, with the love, compassion and care she received from you and from the hospital staff, she recovers enough to allow you to leave her in the hands of the medical profession. Feeling good, you are able to enjoy your holiday knowing that you were prepared to make that sacrifice for someone you loved.

Affirmation: I am prepared to make sacrifices to help others.

134

❧

Sarcasm

Sarcasm is the lowest form of wit,
and the highest form of vulgarity.

ANON

I F YOU HAVE TO RESORT to sarcasm, then you need to look at your whole personality structure. Young people are sarcastic when they feel threatened, but the sooner this phase is put behind them the better, because it shows clearly that they have little intellect. Such remarks, although they may hit the mark, are distasteful, hurtful, and can bring friendships to an end. If you can't say something nice, don't say anything at all.

Visualisation: You have a friend who is known for his sarcasm. Those who are afraid of his bitter tongue pretend to be his friend, but when secret popularity polls are held amongst his peers, everyone realises he is not rated at all. It is only then that his contemporaries acknowledge that he is not worthy of their time. Alone and bitter, he leaves, and the atmosphere is recharged with positive energy and companionship.

Affirmation: Sarcasm is the lowest form of wit.

135

❧

Screaming

His hilarity was like a scream from a crevasse.

GRAHAM GREENE
1904–1991

SCREAMING IS GOOD FOR YOU, in small doses, but if it becomes a normal thing in your everyday life then there is something very wrong.

Because I have clairvoyant vision of mind energy, I have been able to study the beneficial effects of screaming. The mind energy expands, lifting the pressure from the mind and releasing tensions throughout the body. However, when taken to extremes it can cause hysteria, which brings its own problems. This is because when the mind is far out of the body, other negative energies can take over. This also happens with alcohol and drugs. So if things are getting you down, or you are grieving, have a short sharp scream to release the blockages, and then stop. If you are naturally bad tempered, screaming may be a way of releasing your negative energies, but could cause havoc with your health, and turn away those who are your nearest and dearest. It is a dangerous path, so do try to find a calming influence in your life.

Young people who spend hours screaming at their pop idols should be careful, because when it is prolonged and alongside hundreds of others, hysteria can spread. This in turn causes violent reactions, and then anything can happen. It can also take away the ability to think clearly, and at this stage you could be persuaded to take drugs, which in your normal frame of mind you would reject. So do be careful. If you want to scream, remember to stop and breathe deeply every now and again so that you will always be in control.

Visualisation: **You have just lost someone you love and, heartbroken, you can feel pressure building up around your heart and lungs. You have never screamed before, but you do it now, for your health and safety. You feel the pressure leave, and you relax.**

Affirmation: I might scream now and then, if it is really necessary.

136

❧

Self

The spirit is the true self.

CICERO
106–43 BC

MEDITATION IS THE EASIEST WAY to communicate with the self. The mind expands and touches other dimensions where all things are known. Sometimes, having a mirror image of yourself can be painful, but once you know your true self you are better able to deal with personal problems.

Your imagination will also be strengthened by meditation, enabling you to visualise and picture your own future – which, in time, can be brought through into this dimension. But you must have absolute faith in your own abilities.

Above all, *to thine own self be true*. This is not as easy as it sounds, but is well worth the effort.

Visualisation: Whilst meditating, you are given an image of yourself that seems entirely foreign. You reject this picture immediately, but later, in the privacy of your own room, you think about it, and realise that there is a side to you that you dislike and which you have tried to ignore. The experience has been painful, but you take a private oath to deal with your weaknesses.

Affirmation: Know thyself.

137

❧

Self-esteem

*Oft-times nothing profits more
Than self-esteem, grounded on just and right
Well manag'd.*

JOHN MILTON
1608–1674

IF YOU HAVE SELF-ESTEEM you can manage your life, secure in the knowledge that your intuitive words and actions are serving you well. It is not always easy to hold on to self-esteem when everything about us is falling apart, but it is at these times that we need it most. In retrospect, we can see how well it has served us, reducing the tensions and enabling us to think clearly, and we feel reassured and know that we will continue to make the right decisions and keep our self-esteem.

It is about spirituality and our higher self.

Visualisation: You have always tried to live by spiritual values, but when acquaintances mock you for it, you are tempted to deny your own beliefs in order to retain your popularity. However, when you are alone you know that you are selling yourself short, and that you are worth more. With this knowledge comes a sense of peace. The next time it happens, you acknowledge their mocking with a smile, and say, 'Well, it would be a boring old world if we were all alike, wouldn't it?' No one can argue with that!

Affirmation: My self-esteem is high. I feel good!

138

❧

Self-importance

*You may think that you are important,
but there are billions of people out there
who don't give a damn.*

BETTY SHINE

PEOPLE WHO ARE SELF-IMPORTANT are irritating, to say the least. They should look around and study those who are successful human beings, who have caring and loving relationships with friends and family. Self-importance isolates you from people, until friends become a thing of the past.

If you have been told that you fit into this category, take the advice seriously, because you could be doing great harm to your health and your future.

Visualisation: Your promotion to managing director has gone to your head. It is not long before you realise that the easy-going relationship you had with your fellow workers has disappeared for, although they are polite, the warmth has gone. Worse – they try to avoid you. Your self-importance may make *you* feel good, but it is an embarrassment to those who knew you before your promotion.

Fortunately, a close friend brings you down to earth with some practical advice. It takes time, but you do eventually renew your friendships and learn to administrate without the pompous attitude.

Affirmation: Self-importance is an embarrassment to others.

139

❦

Self-indulgence

The way in which the man of genius rules is by persuading an efficient minority to coerce an indifferent and self-indulgent majority.

SIR JAMES FITZJAMES STEPHEN
1829–1894

SELF-INDULGENCE IS A CRIME against yourself, giving in to the weaker side of your character because you are too lazy to do otherwise. Self-indulgent people are difficult to live with and difficult to work with, as they are unable, for whatever reason, to think of anyone but themselves. *They* are the most important human being in *their own eyes*, and nobody else matters to them. They are a burden to society. The fewer self-indulgent people we have around, the better.

The only way a self-indulgent person can change is if *they* want to.

Visualisation: You are worried about your health. Your partner, who is overweight, selfish, pleasure-seeking, and self-absorbed, doesn't care about your feelings, or that his attitude is affecting your health. Eating is his main hobby, and you have to provide the food and run around after him.

One day, after a visit to your doctor, you realise that nothing will ever change unless you do something about it. When you arrive home you leave a note in the kitchen. 'If you want a meal, cook it, and if you don't change I am leaving.' Then you map out a life for yourself that will take you away from the home as much as possible. It may or may not work, but *you* are going to get yourself a life.

Affirmation: I do not have to dance to the tune of self-indulgent people.

140

❧

Self-pity

My prime of youth is but a frost of cares;
My feast of joy is but a dish of pain;
My crop of corn is but a field of tares;
And all my good is but vain hope of gain.
The day is past, and yet I saw no sun;
And now I live, and now my life is done.

CHIDIOCK TICHBORNE
*c.*1558–1586

Tichborne wrote his *elegy* in the Tower of London before his execution. He had every right to indulge in self-pity, but the rest of us, who regularly treat ourselves to a dose of this very negative emotion for unimportant matters, should shake ourselves and thank God, because things could be a lot worse.

Fatigue is our greatest enemy, because when we are tired we feel unable to deal with even the smallest problems, and it is at this point that we sit down and drown ourselves in waves of self-pity. So do try to combat fatigue by taking time off to relax.

Rejection is another major cause for self-pity. In fact, there are a million reasons for indulging in this emotion, both major and minor, and the hurt one feels for oneself can be overwhelming. But there are millions of people all over the world who are suffering the same intense feelings. Try not to indulge for more than five minutes at a time. By breaking it up like this you stop the molehill growing into a mountain.

We are not islands, we are part of a whole Universe of Energy where the minds of others, who are long gone from this dimension, care about you. You are not alone.

Visualisation: **Your life, at this moment, is a misery. Everything seems to have gone wrong and you are indulging in a prolonged bout of self-pity. Suddenly, you become aware of a small blue light dancing around your head. Fascinated, you forget your problems as your eyes follow the light around, watching it expand to the size of a tennis ball and then becoming a mere pin-point, twinkling like a small sapphire. A timely reminder that help is always at hand. With that knowledge and your equilibrium restored, you are determined to show the world that you do have the courage and strength to carry you through the difficult times.**

Affirmation: I am not alone. Someone, somewhere, cares about me.

141

❧

Sensationalism

The chapter on the Fall of the Rupee you may omit.
It is somewhat too sensational.

OSCAR WILDE
1854–1900

SENSATIONALISM MAKES A NONSENSE out of most things, but in dealing with the paranormal it is most important to avoid it, both in the profession and outside of it.

I have tried to put it into perspective in my books, and have simplified this very difficult subject so that everyone can understand what it is all about. But I am sometimes interviewed by newspaper journalists who want sensationalism, because that is what *their* job is all about. I think that the press should be truthful and more realistic about the paranormal, because I have had letters from countless people all over the world, who have accepted the fact that there are things that they do not understand, but who are willing to listen to someone who practises in this field every day. They are learning, and they are practising, and they are being successful, but they are not looking for sensationalism because they know that nothing works without that essential ingredient – spirituality.

There are many tragic things happening every day in our society which are sensationalised. Wrong-doings are bad enough, without making them worse, and giving criminals so much space in our newspapers does little to help this growing problem.

Children nowadays are being born into a world of high adrenaline attitudes and atmospheres. This is unhealthy and dangerous. This attitude must change if we are to teach our children not to sensationalise every little thing that happens in their lives.

Visualisation: **Having worked as a journalist for many years, you are sick of reading sensational stories that have been born out of someone else's sorrow, and you decide to write in a simple and truthful way. Your editor is not amused, but after much argument he agrees to give you a three-month trial period with your own column. Within weeks you are receiving letters from people who have found your column refreshing and peaceful. It is a great success. Your editor, slightly put out, admits defeat, and makes the column a permanent feature.**

Only a small victory you might say, but a victory nevertheless.

Affirmation: Truth and simplicity are the name of the game.

142

Sensitivity

I shook the habit off
Entirely and for ever, and again
In Nature's presence stood, as now I stand,
A sensitive being, a creative soul.

WILLIAM WORDSWORTH
1770–1850

SENSITIVITY CAN BE A CURSE as well as a blessing. If you are too sensitive you will find life difficult until you have learnt to deal with it. An ability to laugh at yourself is a great protection against the hurtful words and actions that may be directed towards you. Do not try to change others to suit your sensitive nature, because there are many more who will take their place. The remedy lies within *you*. If you are really suffering, have a good cry to get over it, and then get on with your life. Nobody is worth the anguish. There is a life out there for you and, armed with the knowledge that your sense of humour grows stronger with the years, you will succeed.

If it is any help, sensitivity does take second place when you have to fight for your existence. Work also is a great leveller, because when you simply do not have the time to indulge in hurt feelings, they have to go.

Visualisation: Because you have always been extremely sensitive, you have become a loner. This is the easiest way, you believe, to protect yourself from the outside world.

One day, whilst placing flowers on a friend's grave, you are drawn towards another headstone, on it you read:

> From quiet homes and first beginning
> Out to the undiscovered ends,
> There's nothing worth the wear of winning,
> But laughter and the love of friends.

HILAIRE BELLOC 1870–1953

As you stand looking at the quotation, you are overcome with emotion, and realise how much you are missing by shutting out the laughter and love of friends. You also know that someone has guided you to that particular stone. Warmed by this thought you leave, knowing that you will find a way to handle your sensitivity.

Affirmation: If I am hurt, I will ride the crest of the wave. It has to beach itself sometime.

143
❧

Sexual harassment

The soft, unhappy sex.

Mrs Aphra Behn
1640–1689

SEXUAL HARASSMENT IS A CRIME, and the perpetrator should be dealt with immediately. There can be no excuse for anyone who invades another person's space in this way. Man or woman, they have to be stopped, otherwise someone else who may be even weaker will have to face the same torment. If you find yourself on the receiving end of sexual harassment, protect yourself by sharing your experiences with a counsellor, and make sure that the person who is committing this crime knows that you are doing so. Do not, in any circumstances, keep this experience to yourself. The more people who know, the safer you will be.

Visualisation: You have been promoted and have been given an office to yourself. Unfortunately, your boss seems to think that this is an invitation for him to sexually harass you. Not wishing to lose your job, you keep quiet. In the ensuing months your health fails and you are demoted. However, the same thing happens to the next in line for promotion, but she is a feisty lady and not only kicks him in the shins but reports him to the chairman. She wins her case, her boss is dismissed, and she makes a success of her appointment.

You are angry that through your own timidity you have lost out, and promise yourself that if it ever happens to you again you will be strong and unmask the person concerned. The good news, though, is that the chairman has been informed of the facts regarding your experiences and you are given a second chance in another office.

Courage is the name of the game. Nothing is worth the humiliation of being sexually harassed.

Affirmation: I will protect myself at all costs, and fight for my rights.

144

❖

Shouting

Every man shouting in proportion to
the amount of his subscription.

R. S. SURTEES
1803–1864

SHOUTING REALLY IS A WASTE OF TIME, because your message becomes a blurred noise, and the impact that you wish to have is lost. It is also extremely painful and unpleasant to be around people who shout all the time. The noise gives you a headache that makes you want to leave at the first opportunity.

Television programmes that depict shouting matches give children the impression that they have *carte blanche* to act in the same manner, and they become immune to it. Likewise, animals do not understand our language, so do not shout at them. They react to kindness and love, whereas shouting simply causes problems later when, having become used to the noise, they ignore it.

The only time that shouting is justified is when you are warning someone of danger, or participating in some way in sport or games that induce high spirits. Otherwise curb the noise, calm down, and get your point home with intelligent conversation.

It is also true that shouting causes vibrations that interfere with the immune system, so do be careful.

Visualisation: You are continually shouting at your children and the dog, so when you take them for a walk in the local park no amount of shouting brings them back to your side, even though they are in danger. A passer-by suggests that you buy a dog whistle to train the dog to return, and when this has been accomplished, that you teach the children to use it so that they remain by your side at all times. You try it and it works. You also stop shouting at home because, for the first time in your life, you realise that you are wasting valuable energy which you need for your own survival.

Your home becomes a haven for your partner too, as instead of a disturbed atmosphere there is peace and contentment, and everyone is happy.

Affirmation: I will re-educate myself not to shout.

145

❧

Showers

She said no more and as she turned away
there was a bright glimpse of the rosy glow of her
neck, and from her ambrosial head of hair a heavenly
fragrance wafted;
her dress flowed down right to her feet, and in her
walk it showed,
she was in truth a goddess.

VIRGIL
70–19 BC

W HEN THE DAY IS DONE and we return home tired and crumpled, there is nothing as refreshing as a shower. Standing with the warm cascading water caressing your body, you can feel the tensions evaporate, and peace is restored. It imitates the effect of nature's rain showers – that feeling of cleanliness as dust and grime are washed away and natural colours regain their healthy sheen.

Those of us who live in a country where water is plentiful cannot wholly appreciate what a priceless commodity it is. The appalling conditions in countries that have continual droughts can only be imagined. We must never take it for granted – and one of the greatest benefits of showers of course is that they lower the consumption of water.

If you don't have a shower, or one of the many attachments that can be fixed to both taps, try the next exercise.

Visualisation: **You are continually annoyed by the fact that other members of your family hog the bathroom. Sitting around moping, you start to build up a picture of yourself under a shower. This experience is so intense, that you can feel the water flowing over your body, washing away the tensions. Your mind, for once, is peaceful, and you feel wonderful.**

When you are at last allowed into the bathroom, you know that bathing will be more intense and satisfying for this experience.

This exercise is also valuable for women in the menopause. When hot flushes invade your body, think of yourself under a cold, cold, shower. It really works! It can also help with those who suffer with skin complaints.

Affirmation: Refreshed and revitalised, I am ready to face the world again.

146

❧

Shrine

Dear Child! dear Girl! that walkest with me here
If thou appear untouched by solemn thought,
Thy nature is not therefore less divine.
Thou liest in Abraham's bosom all the year;
And worshipp'st at the temple's inner shrine,
God being with thee when we know it not.

WILLIAM WORDSWORTH
1770–1850

IN MANY RELIGIONS, shrines are used for focusing attention on spiritual thought, and for this reason they are irreplaceable. Many people have shrines in their homes to remind them of their spiritual values and to enhance the atmosphere.

Shrines also attract phenomena, such as the appearance of tears or holy ash. Because mind energy is absorbed by inanimate objects, the loving thoughts that are projected towards the shrine give it a life of its own, and with an abundance of this power, anything can happen.

Visualisation: You have a shrine that depicts your particular spiritual values. Every day you focus your attention on it, projecting your loving and caring thoughts. After a while you find that by touching it daily your health is enhanced, and you encourage your family to do the same. They also benefit, because as each individual mind projects loving and healing thoughts, the shrine becomes even more powerful and the atmosphere in the home more peaceful.

Affirmation: A shrine can reflect a mirror image of yourself by the vibrations it contains.

147

❦

Sign of the Cross

Except ye see signs and wonders, ye will not believe.

THE BIBLE, ST JOHN

THE SIGN OF THE CROSS has always worked for me, and for my clients, as a symbol of peace. If you have sleeping problems, make the sign of the cross on yourself, the door of your bedroom, and on your bed head or pillow. It was quite by accident that I found that this worked. I was going through some very troubled times many years ago, and when I walked into my bedroom I made the sign on the door, in the room and on the bed head, and I enjoyed the best night's sleep I'd had for many weeks. The next night I forgot to make the sign and I had a lousy night. I never forgot again until the problems were solved. When it first happened, someone was obviously guiding me. I was brought up as a member of the High Church of England, and although I later rejected the church, the symbol has always been a part of my life. It had no meaning however for many of my clients, so when I recommended that they make the sign in their bedrooms to try and overcome their insomnia, they laughed. Humour and a little persuasion, however, did the trick, and they did it for themselves. To their everlasting amazement, it worked! If you have insomnia or any other problems, do try it. You will find that it brings immediate peace.

Visualisation: You have suffered from anxiety for many years, and it seems that nothing can cure it. Then you read that by making the sign of the cross, you will bring yourself peace. Using this sign around your house, you find that your state of mind improves.

Then you receive some worrying news about a member of your family. Immediately, you make the sign and ask for help. Within days, the problem is solved in such a way that it could only have been brought about by an outside influence, and you know that you will never again ignore the power of this sign.

Affirmation: I know that with this sign I will have peace within.

148

❧

Silence

*Under all speech that is good for anything there lies a
silence that is better. Silence is deep as Eternity;
speech is shallow as Time.*

THOMAS CARLYLE
1795–1881

WITHOUT COMPLETE SILENCE I would not be able to work. Through listening to the audible silence of the Universal Mind and the very positive knowledge that I receive from my spiritual teachers through meditation, and from the two-way conversations which give me survival evidence, I know that silence is the key to all these things.

It is also very necessary for your health. The mind, body and spirit all need silence to rejuvenate and regenerate the whole.

Make a special time every day for your silent hour. It will change your life.

Visualisation: Having been ill, you are advised by your doctor to take it easy for a time. Because you are normally a workaholic you become very bored until, one afternoon, sitting quietly in a comfortable armchair, you experience something entirely new to you. Silence. While it wraps itself around you like a warm blanket, you are able, for the first time in your life, to pick up messages of peace, contentment and love from the ether, and you know that in future you will always have time for silence.

Affirmation: I must always make time for silence in my life.

149
❧

Simplification

Our life is frittered away by detail . . . Simplify, simplify.

Henry David Thoreau
1817–1862

M Y MOTTO IS, 'SIMPLIFY'. That is why I have written my books in simple language, so that everyone can understand my explanations and philosophies. So many esoteric books have been written in a language that is a complete mystery to most of us, and that is why it has taken so long for the general public to understand that in the paranormal, we are in fact looking at a science – one that extends outside the limits of *ordinary* science, and one so incredible that it defies belief.

Most people complicate their lives with so many small details that their minds are like rubbish tips. As you think, analyse your thoughts, and then decide which are worthy of your attention and which should be thrown away. Then, when you can give your full attention to those you have retained – simplify. By doing this you can reduce the load.

Visualisation: You are walking along the garden path to gather herbs for the evening dinner. It begins to rain, and you are soon soaked to the skin. You realise that by planting the herbs at the end of the garden, you have deliberately complicated your life. During the next few weeks you move them closer to the house and, in so doing, make things easier for yourself.

Affirmation: Simplify. Simplify. Simplify.

150
❧

Sincerity

*Sir, are you so grossly ignorant of human nature, as
not to know that a man may be very sincere in good
principles, without having good practice?*

SAMUEL JOHNSON
1709–1784

MOST PEOPLE QUICKLY RECOGNISE and avoid those who are insincere. If you cannot be sincere in your feelings when speaking to someone, then keep quiet or change the subject. This is much better than giving out unsettling vibes.

However, there are some people who have such an inferiority complex that they imagine others to be insincere when in fact they are not, so do not judge too quickly.

Sincerity is absolutely essential if you wish to succeed. Nobody likes to be taken for a fool.

Visualisation: **You are listening to an acquaintance telling you how much she hates her neighbour's cat. Much later, you hear her telling the neighbour how she loves her cat. At the next opportunity you ask her why she is so insincere.**

'Well, you have to keep in with the neighbours, don't you?' she replies.

'But why say anything at all?' you ask. 'Isn't it better to keep quiet than to be so insincere? She is not a fool, you know.' Your acquaintance flounces away. As the years passed by, you realise people have avoided her company and she's become a very lonely woman.

You can fool some people, some of the time. But not all the people all the time.

Affirmation: Sincerity is much the best option.

151

❦

Singing

My soul is an enchanted boat,
Which, like a sleeping swan, doth float
Upon the silver waves of thy sweet singing.

PERCY BYSSHE SHELLEY
1792–1822

SINGING IS THE MOST WONDERFUL exercise for the mind and body because it releases all the blockages throughout the system. It is exhilarating, and it doesn't matter one iota whether you have a good voice or not – it is how it makes you feel that is important. If others complain about your singing, don't let them put you off but sing when you are alone. Singing expands the mind, linking you with the universe and healing energies.

Visualisation: It is dawn, and as you lie in bed listening to the chorus of bird song you notice that a blackbird has perched on a branch immediately outside your window. As it sings, an aura of energy appears all around its body. When it stops, the aura gradually fades. However, it stays there long enough for you to be able to observe the startling effect that singing has had on this beautiful bird. As the sun rises it becomes more difficult to see the aura, but you know you will never forget this incredible experience.

Afterwards, it dawns on you that if such a thing can happen to a bird, then it must also happen to humans. The next time you sing, you visualise the colours of the aura around you and see it expanding, and the tensions melt away.

Affirmation: Singing exhilarates, and rejuvenates.

152

❧

Sittings

Let us have a quiet hour,
Let us hob-and-nob with Death.
Every moment dies a man,
Every moment one is born.

ALFRED, LORD TENNYSON
1809–1892

I HAVE ALWAYS FOUND IT quite unbelievable when, upon my giving them survival evidence, the sitter sometimes begins to give me the life-history of the person from the other side who is giving me the evidence. It is very difficult indeed to hear messages when your client cannot stop speaking! These interruptions undoubtedly have an effect on the length of the sitting, because one loses contact with the communicator. I remember one lady who had the most marvellous evidence from her brother, but she reminisced for too long, despite my protests. When she had eventually run out of steam, she couldn't understand why he had gone.

The same thing has happened at small gatherings, when I have been asked to talk and demonstrate healing and mediumship. I remember one time when I had successfully diagnosed someone, he immediately gathered people around him to give his explanation of how it had happened. Giving survival evidence to the same group turned into chaos and my presence became superfluous. They were all executives, and unfortunately thought they knew it all. Sadly, through this kind of exhibitionism, they all lost out.

If you have a sitting and the medium asks you a question, make your answer as concise as possible so that they can get on with the rest of the evidence. There will always be time to converse later when the communicator has left.

Visualisation: **Whilst receiving survival evidence, you are tempted to enlarge on the information that the medium is giving, but you refrain from doing so. During the next few moments you are surprised when this same information is being given to you by the communicator, and you wonder whether the medium is telepathic. However, more facts are added that even you did not know, but you can make sense of the whole – and it is then that you realise that what you are receiving is the truth in its entirety, and which solves a long-standing mystery. Had you interrupted at the beginning of the sitting, you may never have known the answer.**

Affirmation: I will answer questions when required to do so, but I shall endeavour to remain silent until the end of the sitting.

153

❦

Sobbing

Life is made up of sobs, sniffles, and smiles, with sniffles predominating.

O. HENRY
1862–1910

WHEN EMOTIONS ARE HIGH, sobbing can be the end result of a long crying session. Shock can cause immediate sobbing. Persistent pain is another reason. The body, no longer able to retain the pressure, causes a reaction that releases the pent-up emotions, so sobbing can be good for you, in short doses. The problems begin when you have allowed it to go on for so long that you are unable to stop. At this stage, it requires an enormous effort by yourself to curb it slowly until it ends.

Visualisation: You have been sobbing for some time; your body is aching all over and you have a severe headache, but you cannot stop. Then you remember that you have an important engagement the next day that will require you to present yourself at your best. Going to the bathroom you stand under a warm shower and visualise the water soaking up your grief and carrying it away. When that is finished, you rinse your face under a cold tap. You turn on the radio and find some soothing but not sad music, and whilst relaxing on the bed you place some eye pads over your eyes. Then, breathing deeply, you fall asleep. You are at peace once again.

Affirmation: No matter how bad things are, nothing lasts forever.

154

Solitude

For oft, when on my couch I lie
In vacant or in pensive mood,
They flash upon that inward eye
Which is the bliss of solitude;
And then my heart with pleasure fills,
And dances with the daffodils.

WILLIAM WORDSWORTH
1770–1850

SOLITUDE IS A MUST FOR A WRITER, because any kind of noise or interruption can cause one to lose the train of thought, and to an author lost words can cause great sadness. Likewise, it is also essential that healers and mediums have solitude.

When meditating, I have found that solitude gives me a greater advantage than silence, because the messages I receive are clearer. It is possible to meditate with others when silence is preserved, but one is always aware that minds do link with one another. If you can find the solitude needed for great meditation then your efforts will be rewarded.

There are many reasons for seeking solitude, but remember to keep a balance in your life. No matter how important it is to you, do not shut out friends and family. There is a time and place for everything.

Visualisation: Fed up with work and the demands that are being made of you from other sources, you decide to take a long trekking holiday in the Himalayas, arranging to stay overnight in the small monasteries dotted throughout the mountains. Although the days are long and the route difficult, the solitude enables you to interact with the environment. Heavy perfume lingers in the air where no flowers or herbs exist, and you can hear the buzz of voices although no other human is near. In the distance you can see images of animals watching you, and overhead an eagle appears to be guiding you to your destination.

Arriving at a monastery, you are shown into a small room where you are given food and water. Before retiring, a cloaked figure approaches you and places his hand on your shoulder, saying, 'The things you have seen and heard on this journey do exist, but in another world. This has been my gift to you.'

In the morning you ask one of the monks for the identity of this cloaked figure. He looks surprised, then smiles. 'You have been blessed,' he says. 'He is the guardian spirit of travellers, and it is very rare for him to make an appearance.'

Returning home you find that you have been given another gift, that of compassion and peace, which in turn touches everyone you meet.

Affirmation: In my solitude I will touch my soul.

155

Soul

Let knowledge grow from more to more,
But more of reverence in us dwell;
That mind and soul, according well,
May make one music as before.

ALFRED, LORD TENNYSON
1809–1892

I BELIEVE THAT THE MIND *is* the soul. I have seen it leave the physical body, and spin into another dimension.

In my book *Mind to Mind* I explain how the minds of those we have lost link up with the medium's mind and pass on the messages that are the evidence of survival. But I appreciate that other people have different ideas. Whatever your views, I am sure that you will agree that it is very warming to think that we do have a soul, and that it will continue to protect and shield us from the black negative energies that exist in all dimensions.

Visualisation: Having spent most of your life trying to help others, you are regularly reminded of how ungrateful some of these people have been. One day, whilst day-dreaming, you hear someone say, 'You gave willingly of your help because your soul demanded it.' You realise the truth of these words. In every situation you gave because you wanted to give, and you now feel a warm glow when you understand the real significance of the message – that you have a good soul.

Affirmation: My soul dictates the kind of person I am.

156

⁂

Spirits

Move along these shades
In gentleness of heart, with gentle hand
Touch – for there is a spirit in the woods.

WILLIAM WORDSWORTH
1770–1850

SPIRITS ARE EVERYWHERE, inhabiting dimensions that are worlds within worlds. It is sometimes possible to see spirits with our minds, but most of the time we are so earthed by the effort of living that it becomes impossible to imagine, let alone see them. We can sometimes feel the coldness when a spirit is near, and occasionally the hair can stand up on the back of the neck. The reason for this is that they have to draw energy from us to remain in this environment. As a medium I have been able to see spirits most of my life, and still consider it a great honour to have had such an incredible gift bestowed upon me.

For those of you who do not believe in the existence of spirits, or life after death, consider how egotistical it is to believe that we are the only beings in the universe. Remember, we can only see when the energy surrounding a person or object is the same as our energy system. When it is different we are blind.

Visualisation: **You are walking around an ancient religious site when you find yourself surrounded by misty people. They have a transparent but human form. At first, they appear to be interested in you, then you watch as they disperse and go their separate ways, and you realise that you have strayed into their space just as they sometimes stray into ours.**

Because the atoms in all dimensions have so many varied patterns, we should expect paranormal phenomena, spirits and miracle healing when they collide.

Affirmation: The mind is everlasting, therefore we will all become spirits one day.

157

Spirituality

*There is a spirituality about the face, however . . . which
the typewriter does not generate. The lady is a musician.*

SIR ARTHUR CONAN DOYLE
1859–1930

THE MIND IS SPIRIT. Spirituality, however, is how you activate the goodness in your mind/soul for the benefit of mankind. It also refers to knowledge, and how you use that knowledge. Having the courage to combat the evils of this world adds to your spirituality. It is not an easy path to follow, but the love you will feel around you will be your reward.

Visualisation: It is your birthday, but you are sad. You have spent most of your life helping others, yet you are alone with no birthday cards or presents. You wonder why all these people have forsaken you. Then the doorbell rings and, as you open the door, people pour into your home, piling presents on the floor and covering the dining-room table with food and champagne. 'We are returning the love that we have all received from you over the years,' a friend tells you, 'now it is your turn to receive.'

Affirmation: My spirituality will be of my own making.

158
❦

Spite

Only take this rule along,
Always to advise her wrong;
And reprove her when she's right;
She may then grow wise for spite.

JONATHAN SWIFT
1667–1745

S PITEFULNESS IS CRUEL and unnecessary, and underlines the ignorance and low self-esteem of the perpetrator. If you are a victim, walk away from it, because you will never win.

If you are the perpetrator, analyse why you are giving so much grief to others, because whatever the cause you must sort it out. People disappear in droves when they are faced with spite, as they simply cannot handle this vindictive trait – and there is no reason at all why they should.

Visualisation: Looking at a group of teenagers, you notice that one, in particular, is being particularly spiteful. She is using words to hurt and attack the most attractive girl there. The others make no attempt to protect the girl until the spitefulness becomes physical, as words are emphasised with prods and pokes to the body. Then they fill the space between them, demanding an explanation as to why the girl was being abused in this way. 'I don't like her face,' replies the spiteful girl. The answer is received with a groan of derision. 'Well, you're on your own, now we know how jealous and spiteful you can be.' Arm in arm, they all walk away, leaving a very unhappy, lonely girl, who faces complete isolation until she changes her ways.

Affirmation: I must protect myself from spite by walking away.

159

❧

Stability

so much depends
upon

a red wheel
barrow

glazed with rain
water

beside the white
chickens.

WILLIAM CARLOS WILLIAMS
1883 – 1963

IT IS SOMETIMES the little things in life that give us our stability. Children especially like to know that someone is at home when they return from school. Brimming over with all the important things that have happened to them that day, they need to tell someone about them straight away. Young and impatient, they do not want to wait until later, they need you *now*. Those of you who have children will recognise this scenario. If children grow up in a stable home, they will cherish their memories forever and, in turn, these memories will support them when they are most needed.

Adults also need stability in their lives. Some men can become quite aggressive if furniture in the house is moved around – it shows how they felt comfortable and secure in the home, otherwise, the change would not have had this effect.

Similarly, women become particularly annoyed when they go to their favourite supermarket and find that the items on the shelves have been moved around (yet again!) and the shopping takes twice as long as they turn detective trying to find the elusive goods. The feel-good safety factor has gone, and shopping becomes a nightmare. It is especially difficult for those who are infirm or have impaired sight – they lose their stability. Supermarket administrators need to think about this problem.

No matter how many times you may change your circumstances, always maintain some stability for yourself and those around you, even if it is only to assure them that you will always love them. Material things can always come later.

Visualisation: **You return home from university expecting your parents to be at home to welcome you, but they have left a note telling you that they have been called away and will not be back until later. Feeling miserable and rejected, you raid the fridge and prepare a makeshift meal. Later, as you dejectedly drag your bundles up the stairs and open your bedroom door, you are amazed to find that your mother, for once in her life, has not altered your room. It is exactly as you had left it. On your pillow is a note. 'This is your room – your space – and it will always be so. Love, Mum.' The feel-good factor is back.**

Affirmation: I must be earthed so that I can fly.

160

✤

Stealing

*To keep my hands from picking and stealing, and my
tongue from evil-speaking, lying, and slandering.*

PRAYER BOOK
1662

STEALING IS A CRIME against humanity. If you cannot obtain things through hard work and talent, then you have to go without. Find a way to improve your mind and your spirituality so that when you *are* able to afford the materialistic objects you so desire, you may find that you don't want them, having found a more rewarding path. It is delightful to own nice things, but when they do not belong to you, and never will, how can you enjoy them? The spirit of the owner will always inhabit them. Inanimate objects vibrate with unseen energies and the minds of those who loved them, and you will never know peace until they have been restored to their rightful owners.

If you have stolen an animal, it can also link through mind energy with its rightful owner. You will never own them. The power of the mind, of both humans and animals, is far greater than you could ever imagine.

Visualisation: Having stolen a beautiful antique, you place it on a table in your home to admire it. But when you try to touch it, a pain shoots up your arm into your neck and head. Frightened by this inexplicable reaction, you wait a few minutes and try again. The same thing happens. Later that day, you visit a partner in crime and tell him about your experience. He frowns. 'You'll have to give it back,' he says. 'I've known this happen to other people, and they have nothing but grief until they return the piece to its rightful owner.' You dismiss his advice and resolve to keep it.

After months of bad luck, and still getting the same reaction from the antique, you finally decide to return it. Breaking into the house, you are apprehended by the owner. He sees the antique and insists that you tell him the whole story. When you have finished, he says, 'That belonged to my late wife. She loved it, and when she died she told me that I would only have to touch it and she would be there.' He smiles sadly. 'She would have died fighting for that piece – it makes sense that she attacked you through it.' He allows you to leave quietly, but extracts a promise that you never steal again. Relieved, you leave, but you have been taught a valuable lesson. Everything has a mind of its own – so beware!

Affirmation: I will never steal. The things I own must love me.

❧

161

Supernatural

*The strongest man in the world
is the man who stands alone.*

HENRIK IBSEN
1828–1906

SUPER-NATURAL. That is how it should be spelt. It is an extension of *natural* forces that people like myself have the gift to attract, harness and manipulate for the good of mankind.

There are others who are able to harness opposing forces and use them for evil, as with black magic. But in this same natural extension you will find the Law of the Universe, which dictates the rewards or punishments we deserve. Evil-doers never win. They may appear to do so materially, but their minds and physical bodies cannot stand the strain.

To most people, spirits are also super-natural. They are a blueprint of the mind/soul that can be projected from other dimensions to those they wish to visit. To mediums they are a normal and natural sight.

In this sometimes dreary world, it is wonderful to know that super-natural forces do exist, and that one day you may benefit from them.

Visualisation: Having decided to visit a famous monastery, you are amazed when you see a line of monks in the distance, filing towards the old part of the monastery. Then, just before they reach the entrance, they disappear. Entranced by this sight, you turn to a stranger who has appeared at your side, and say, 'Were they ghosts, do you think?'

He laughs. 'Yes, I've seen them several times on my visits to this place. I've been told by those that live near here that the energy the monks bring with them sustains and maintains this place by the number of visitors it attracts.' He touches your arm. 'You have been blessed,' he says. As he walks away, he too disappears.

Affirmation: Blessed are they who believe that all things are possible.

162

❧

Superstition

There is a superstition in avoiding superstition.

FRANCIS BACON
1561–1626

I F YOU ARE SUPERSTITIOUS, then you will surely bring about that which you believe. In your mind you have drawn a blueprint of your beliefs, which are then recorded in your 'mind file', and things will happen as you have instructed them to do. You cannot afford negative thoughts, as they could affect your whole life.

I have known people who will not go out on a certain day of the month, who have to tap every door in the house when they pass it, who will only cross a street at a certain point, and who will not wear a jumper unless they have a vest on inside-out underneath. These superstitions sound ridiculous, but not to the people who have imprisoned themselves within the walls of these beliefs, and who assume that they cannot escape. Walking under ladders is a common superstition, but when you look at it logically, you are more likely to be hit by falling debris if you walk around them – you could even be hit by a car as you step off the pavement! Unfortunately, these arguments do not hold any weight when you are talking to someone who has turned their superstitions into a religion. At some time, though, you have to free yourself from these fears. They take away freedom of thought, word and deed, because you believe that you have no choice. You *always* have a choice!

Visualisation: **You are in a garden where, for safety, you are building a high wall around yourself. One day a figure appears beside you. He tells you that the high walls are not a protection at all, but a prison. He places his hand against the middle of the wall and miraculously pulls out a brick. 'Come,' he says. 'Look through this space and tell me what you see.' As you look through the hole in the wall, you see a most beautiful landscape, an abundance of brightly coloured flowers, animals, birds and butterflies and sunshine radiating from a deep blue sky. 'There is life out there,' the stranger whispers in your ear. 'Here you have nothing. You must remove all the bricks from this wall and let the light shine into your heart and mind. Allow yourself to live without fear, for fear is a darkness we cannot afford.'**

Affirmation: There is no place for superstition in my life.

163

❧

Survival

I survived.

Abbé Emmanuel Joseph Sieyès
1748–1836

IN LIFE YOU SIMPLY cannot give up, no matter how bad things are. We all have our own in-built survival kit that will help us in desperate circumstances. Surviving has very little to do with courage but a lot to do with choice, and only we can choose whether to fight or not. Usually we are on our own when these decisions have to be made, and it is this isolation that makes or breaks the individual. However, when we have made the right choice and have survived, the joy is indescribable, and we can be proud of our achievement. Our compassion and understanding are also heightened, and this in turn, can benefit mankind.

Visualisation: You have been left with two small children and very little money. Looking around your flat with its small balcony, you write down your options, and then decide to grow as many life-giving vegetables as possible. Visiting friends, you ask them to donate all sizes of flower pots, which you gather together on the balcony. With a small sum of money you buy the seeds. By rotating the sowing times, you have fresh salads and herbs throughout the summer, plus new potatoes which you've grown in a plastic sack. In winter, you bring the herbs indoors and keep them on the window-sill, along with mustard and cress which is growing in egg containers, and bean sprouts which are growing on cotton wool; you grow winter vegetables outside.

Your achievements become well-known and your local paper publishes your story. You are then asked to give lectures, and this in turn leads to you writing your own books.

Having had very little time to think of yourself, you are quietly pleased one morning when you realise that by hard work and imagination you have carved out a career for yourself, and that you and your children have survived.

Affirmation: I will survive.

164

❦

Symbolism

We are symbols, and inhabit symbols.

RALPH WALDO EMERSON
1803–1882

WE ARE INITIATED into symbolism from birth, mainly through the religious beliefs of our parents. If such beliefs are absent then the symbols could come via sports or private examples conjured up in the mind of a family member. One way or another, there is no doubt that you will be initiated into a symbolic world at some time, and in time will make your own.

Strangely enough, symbolism works. With our own private symbols we make major decisions, hold on to the image for support when times are bad, and hail them as our saviours when the good times reappear.

The cross, of course, is a symbol of peace and spirituality, and is *the* major symbol in the world. Symbolism plays a major role in the world of magic and mystery. In fact, there are symbols everywhere we look – major industries use them in their logos.

To all of you whose symbols work for you, I would say, 'Hold that dream,' because dreams can come true. If however you have negative symbols because of a depressed state of mind, blot them out and get rid of them.

Visualisation: **Still a child, you tell your mother that you have seen a black cat in your dreams. Your mother says that it is a good omen and that something wonderful will happen. Later that day your father arrives home with a bicycle, something you have dreamed of for a long time. Throughout your life the black cat, live and symbolic, brings you good fortune. It was a trigger that sparked positive thought, which, in turn, led to success.**

Affirmation: Symbolism is the positive spark that ignites the mind, to seek and find.

165

❧

Sympathy

It is the secret sympathy,
The silver link, the silken tie,
Which heart to heart, and mind to mind,
In body and soul can bind.

SIR WALTER SCOTT
1771–1832

WE ALL NEED TO FEEL the sympathy of our friends when we hit a bad patch in our lives. If friends are affected at the same time as ourselves, such as in the loss of a loved one, then it is gratifying to receive the silent sympathy they are giving out. To know that we are not alone in times of stress can remove some of the impact of what we are experiencing, and aids recovery.

Sympathy is not the same as feeling sorry for someone. It is a warmth so deep it can be felt, almost touched, that wells up from the heart and envelops the mind and body of the one who is distressed. It is an emotion that we would not wish to be without, and for which we are always truly grateful.

To those of you who have a loving compassionate nature and give sympathy where and when it is needed – thank you.

Visualisation: You have lost a loved one and, in your grief, decide to visit your nearest spiritual centre. It is empty, and as the tears flow, a Being of Light appears, and says, 'Be calm, for I am with you always.' Then it fades and you are alone again. Shaken, you sit quietly, trying to conjure up the image in your mind – to relive the experience – but it is not to be. But you know that the sympathetic aura that had enfolded and embraced you in that moment, along with the words, will be with you forever.

Affirmation: Sympathy is indescribable, and our lives are enhanced by it.

166

Tears

With the persuasive language of a tear.

<small>CHARLES CHURCHILL</small>
1731–1764

I AM SURE that you have heard, for a variety of reasons, the phrase, 'There will be tears before bedtime.' Children use tears of persuasion all the time. If they continue to get away with this infantile behaviour in their teens then, as adults, they will become a drain on their family and friends.

Tears that well up in our hearts through tragedy are different, however. They are a safety valve for the emotional pressures that threaten to destroy our health.

It has been known for many years, that tears rid our bodies of harmful chemicals, and in that respect crying has a healing effect. It is when the tears fall over an extended period and are not controlled that other problems begin. Sinuses become inflamed and infected, the immune system is weakened and we become victims of flu and viruses. At some time during your sad periods, therefore, you must find the necessary discipline to stop. As in all things, there has to be balance.

Visualisation: **You are feeling down, and reliving old wounds. Tears begin to flow and your imagination works overtime as you indulge yourself, remembering the negative moments in your life. Unable to stop crying, your eyes swell, your sinuses hurt and you realise that you have trapped yourself in a vacuum of misery. Unable to see the light because of the self-inflicted depression, you cannot find the path that will lead you out of the darkness. Then you notice a small blue light hovering around the room, and you remember that you had asked a friend for distant healing. Convinced that the phenomenon is due to the help she is giving, you dial her number. She has left a message on her answerphone. 'I am healing at the moment, but please leave your number and I will call you back.' Within minutes you are feeling better, the tears have stopped, and you are reminded of something your friend had said the last time you had spoken to her. 'Remember, we are never alone. And if you ask for help, you will receive it. Above all, have faith.'**

Affirmation: Tears may flow, but – as in all things – there should be a limit.

167

❧

Teasing

Speak roughly to your little boy,
And beat him when he sneezes;
He only does it to annoy,
Because he knows it teases.

LEWIS CARROLL
1832–1898

TEASING CAN BE the act of a friend to induce laughter. It can also be cruel. It depends entirely on the nature of the person who is doing the teasing. Cruel teasing is unwarranted and unnecessary, and is a flaw in the character of the perpetrator. They are usually unhappy people who seek revenge for imagined injustices. Children can sometimes be the most cruel of all, and the parent or carer must deal with this behaviour immediately.

Kind teasing is an excellent way of bringing laughter into someone's life, especially if they are feeling low.

Visualisation: You have two children – your little girl is playing happily with her dolls in the garden when her brother comes along with two friends and teases her. They laugh as she begins to cry, and their teasing becomes merciless as they realise they have total control of her emotions. You have been keeping an eye on them from a distance, and you walk towards them, asking them all to sit on the grass. You sit down beside them and address your son. 'I'm worried about you,' you say. 'You seem to take delight in making your sister unhappy.' The boy looks down, ashamed. 'It is only sad and bad people who behave in this way,' you continue. 'You must find out why you act like this so that we can work it out together.' You turn to the other boys. 'You also have things to work out for yourselves.' You take your little girl by the hand. 'We're leaving now,' you tell the boys, 'because hateful people make us sad and we want to be happy.'

Affirmation: Tease only when it brings happiness to others.

168

❧

Temper

*A tart temper never mellows with age,
and a sharp tongue is the only edged tool that grows keener
with constant use.*

WASHINGTON IRVING
1783–1859

GETTING INTO A TEMPER might relieve stress, but it really does not achieve much. People usually walk away, unable to take the vicious vibes that are being projected. Words are meaningless, because with such anger all logical thought deteriorates.

We all lose our temper at one time or another, because we have to live and work with others if we do not want to be isolated, and their behaviour can have a detrimental effect on our moods. We also live in a materialistic world, always striving for something we do not own, and the effort needed to acquire these things puts us under pressure. The mind, unable to contain this pressure, explodes in a fit of temper. The sad thing is that we do not need most of the objects that we desire. Is it any wonder that children who are indoctrinated into materialism at a very young age, by designer clothes and expensive toys, fly into a fit of temper when they cannot have the object of the latest craze?

If you have a really bad temper, contact a registered hypnotherapist and try to discover the root cause, because there must be one. You do need help because bad tempers can cause terrible problems, and some of them could ruin not only your life but also the lives of those around you.

Visualisation: **Someone in your family is bored, and to combat that boredom they are trying to annoy you. You ignore all their stupid remarks until they say something hurtful about your appearance. You can feel the pressure building up in your mind and body; your violent thoughts are threatening to get out of hand, and you feel out of control as though you are going to explode. Recognising the danger, you put on your coat, walk out of the door, and remove yourself from a potentially violent situation. Slowly, you feel the tensions leave, and your mind and body return to normal. Feeling better, you visit a friend and spend the rest of the day in an amicable atmosphere.**

This exercise may seem as though you are giving in. You are! You cannot combat stupidity if someone is bent on bringing out the worst in you. But you do not have to stoop to their level.

Affirmation: I will not lose my temper. I will keep my self-respect.

169

Temperament

And now I see with eye serene,
The very pulse of the machine;
A being breathing thoughtful breath,
A traveller betwixt life and death;
The reason firm, the temperate will,
Endurance, foresight, strength and skill;
A perfect woman, nobly planned,
To warn, to comfort, and command;
And yet a spirit still, and bright
With something of angelic light.

WILLIAM WORDSWORTH
1770–1850

IF YOU HAVE A FRIEND with an even temperament, then count your blessings. It is wonderful to know that you have someone with whom you can confide. Count your blessings too if *you* have an even temperament, because you will experience more peace, contentment and goodwill than those who have not.

If you are an extrovert personality, inclined to have highs and lows and explode occasionally, then someone with a pleasant, even temperament might irritate you. But remember, it is not their problem, it is yours. So do keep things in perspective.

Visualisation: You have been working hard in a noisy environment and on your free day decide to stay at home, away from any aggravation. Frustrated when the doorbell rings, you go to the door with some trepidation, believing that the peaceful atmosphere you've created is about to disappear. You are not happy. When you open the door, however, you are faced with the only person that you know who will not disturb your peace – your great-aunt. Your frustration turns to delight, and you spend a wonderful, enlightening day with her. When she leaves, you can almost touch the peace that she has left behind, and you know that no one will ever close their doors to her, and she will never be alone.

Affirmation: I will endeavour to even out my temperament.

170

❧

Thought

This gray spirit yearning in desire
To follow knowledge like a sinking star,
Beyond the utmost bound of human thought.

ALFRED, LORD TENNYSON
1809–1892

WE NEED TIME TO THINK. Our thoughts are the most precious thing we have, which is why we are annoyed when our thought processes are interrupted by mundane problems. It is imperative that we find time to think, because doing so expands the mind, enabling us to reach out and touch the hidden knowledge that is contained in the Universal Mind, from which we receive inspiration and the strength to energise our resolve and talents. Thoughts also trigger the imagination, enabling us to enhance and bring to life hitherto unseen images. It is imperative that we take the time to think, for without thought, we will find ourselves in a grey place.

Visualisation: You have to make a long train journey which involves changing at three stations. Not wishing to have any hitches, you sit down and mentally work each required action, from the time you fill your suitcase until you reach your destination. Whilst you are thinking this through, problems that you had been unaware of spring to mind which, if they are not resolved, could cause havoc. You continue this process until you feel that you have covered every aspect of the journey. When you have finished the exercise you know that you have done all you can to avoid any problems and if any *do* arise they will not be of your making.

Affirmation: I cannot reach a conclusion without proper thought.

171

❧

Threats

Breathing out threatenings and slaughter.

THE BIBLE, ACTS OF THE APOSTLES

IGNORANCE AND AN INFERIORITY COMPLEX are the main reasons for people indulging in threatening behaviour. Unable to converse adequately, they torment their victims instead. Not only do these people become inhuman over the years, but I have found that their ugly natures create indelible lines in their faces, and they are easily recognisable.

If you are threatened and you are able to walk away from the situation, do so.

If you see someone else being threatened, get help. It is very dangerous nowadays to intervene personally, unless you have been trained in survival techniques. Most people look the other way when someone else is threatened. This is also wrong. An effort must be made to find the right kind of help. It is not always easy, but there is always *something* one can do in these circumstances without getting yourself injured or killed.

If you have a threatening nature, stop it in its tracks. You will never be happy, fulfilled, or successful in any section of your life if you continue to abuse others in this way. Get an education so that you can meet people on their own level. You must have some good qualities hidden away – find them, work on them, strengthen them. Get a life and stop interfering in the lives of others!

Visualisation: You have been promoted, and are settling into your new office when your predecessor enters, threatening to throw all of your belongings out of the door. 'You don't take over until *I* am ready,' he shouts. Shocked, you leave the room and seek assistance.

When he has been dealt with by other members of the staff, your immediate boss says, 'You were wise to leave him to us. He lost his job because of his violent behaviour, and he could have hurt you.'

If you can walk away, do so.

Affirmation: Ignorance and an inferiority complex are the main causes of threatening behaviour.

172

~

Tolerance

The various modes of worship, which prevailed in the Roman world, were all considered by the people as equally true; by the philosopher, as equally false; and by the magistrate, as equally useful. And thus toleration produced not only mutual indulgence, but even religious concord.

EDWARD GIBBON
1737–1794

TOLERANCE IS A VIRTUE that could be practised more often than it is. Unfortunately, it is very difficult to be tolerant when circumstances are desperate so there is an awful lot of intolerance around. It would make life a lot easier if we could harness and discipline our thoughts. When someone professes to want to help and then seemingly ignores everything we have to say, remember that they too may have overwhelming problems that make it difficult for them to concentrate, no matter how sympathetic they might want to be.

Try to look at the problems you have with others by reversing the situation. This process brings many things to light, and one of them might be your own intolerance. Think before you speak or act. It only takes a minute.

Visualisation: **You have been walking in the country for two hours, seeking a peaceful place to relax and enjoy the small picnic that you have prepared for yourself. The path eventually opens out, and before you lies the most exquisite lake. As the sunlight touches the ripples of water, you know you have found the perfect spot. Lying on the grass, looking into the vastness of the sky and beyond, you feel the tensions of the past year leaving, and you relax. You have time to think, time to look around and observe nature at its best.**

The sound of noisy laughter and dogs barking in the distance ends the silence. Irritated, you feel all the tensions return. As the party arrives at the lakeside, you watch as the children spin stones along the surface of the water, encouraging the dogs to swim after them. A man appears at your side. 'Sorry about the noise,' he says. 'We'll be moving along soon.' Encouraged by his understanding of your situation, you give an amicable nod. He then tells you that he is worried about his children constantly watching television and playing with computers. 'I've brought them out to show them the real world, nature at its best, and to get some fresh air.' Contrite, you tell him that you don't mind how long they stay, that you understand. He thanks you and walks away.

Reminiscing later, you realise that the kindness of one person to another can reveal a tolerance, hitherto unknown.

Affirmation: I will try to be more tolerant of others.

173

❧

Touch

We must touch his weaknesses with a delicate hand.
There are some faults so nearly allied to excellence,
that we can scarce weed out the fault without
eradicating the virtue.

OLIVER GOLDSMITH
1730–1774

As a healer, I am probably more aware of the incredible value of touch than most people. It is only by touching others that we can pass on and receive healing energies that revitalise, renew, and touch our hearts, knowing that someone cares.

It seems that people who live in cold climates are more reserved, and do not touch and hug one another as much as they should. In warm climates, however, people are more relaxed, for as the sun eases away aches and pains they become more amiable, more able to reach out and lend a helping hand.

Because of the violent world we live in today, children are encouraged to resist touch by strangers. This makes sense, but they should also be encouraged to give a loving touch to trusted family members and other children. The best way to do this is to teach them to heal, to place their hands on their mother's head to ease a headache, to gently touch any member of the family in pain. This also shows them that you consider them to be a respected family member, and that their sympathy and understanding are valued. It teaches them to give.

Nothing can replace a loving touch on the arm when we are distressed, a finger touching our face, or, better still, both arms around us in a loving hug. These actions are priceless.

The healing touch of Jesus is well known. He was trying to teach us the power of compassion. Spirituality is about passing on knowledge for the benefit of others. But still, after all this time, there are those who prefer to close their ears and eyes, and who still prefer to walk in the dark.

Visualisation: **You are depressed because you cannot afford to buy your ailing mother a present. 'I have no money,' you tell her. When she explains that she would rather have healing from your hands than a bought gift, you smile, 'Okay, that's what I'll give you,' you reply. Later, when your mother has recovered, she tells you that it was the best present she has ever received.**

Affirmation: I will use touch to enhance the life of others.

174

Tradition

*Tradition means giving votes to the most obscure of
all classes, our ancestors. It is the democracy of the dead.
Tradition refuses to submit to the small and arrogant oligarchy
of those who merely happen to be walking about.
All democrats object to men being disqualified by the
accident of birth;
tradition objects to their being disqualified by the
accident of death.*

G. K. CHESTERTON
1874–1936

TRADITIONS ARE KEPT ALIVE for many reasons. For good or ill, they will always be with us. Pleasant, harmless traditions are a joy and give one a sense of belonging, but when tradition invokes violence, it is being abused.

In this ever-changing world, tradition is always constant, but changes do have to be made. We cannot walk forever in the path of our ancestors; what suited them in their time does not necessarily fit in with life as we know it now. Religious traditions in particular have stayed the same for thousands of years, and yet the world is changing all the time. Surely, these rules and regulations were not meant to stay the same forever. If our ancestors could change the rules, then so can we.

We should keep the best aspects of our traditions and rid ourselves of the worst. Only then can we be proud of our beliefs.

Visualisation: **It is the tradition in your family that, no matter where they may be, they are expected to pay their respects to the head of the clan every year. In some cases this involves air travel. Thoroughly fed up with this annual event, some members decide to bend the rules and visit only every two years. This splits the family. Then the head of the clan tells them that he is thoroughly fed up with their feuding, and he has therefore decided to change the rules. They will not have to visit, but every family will have to keep an account of their lives during the past year, and send it to him. If they wish to visit, they can do so in their own time. 'But it is our tradition to visit at the same time,' they argue. The old man smiles. 'Well, the tradition has been changed. One day I will be an ancestor, and the children of the future will thank me for it.' The wisdom of age has overcome the ignorance of youth.**

Affirmation: Tradition should be a joy. When it is a misery, it must be changed.

175

❧

Tragedy

The bad end unhappily, the good unluckily.
That is what tragedy means.

TOM STOPPARD
1937–

SOME PEOPLE CAN GO through life without experiencing one single tragedy, while others have tragedies heaped upon them, and there seems to be no rhyme or reason why this should be. We try to find some common factor that links the tragedies, to make sense of the grief, but in the end we have to live with the aftermath, and that is the difficulty. Should we shut ourselves away to grieve in private, or seek the company of close friends so that we can talk about it? Or perhaps become a workaholic so that our thoughts cannot invade and destroy us completely? In truth it would be most sensible to do a little of all these things. The choice is yours and we must not be pushed into a corner by others – they will be experiencing their own unique reaction, different from your own. Go with the flow of your emotions. The river of life will eventually carry you into calmer waters.

Visualisation: **You are experiencing the worst tragedy of your life and you feel the need to get away from the emotions of others, which are dragging you down into greater depths of despair. You decide to write a poem about the loved one you have lost and the grief you are experiencing. Locking yourself away, you sit and begin to write. Then you feel the pressure of a hand on your shoulder, and find that you are writing words before they have impinged on your mind. When you have finished you look at the paper, which reads:**

> *I am here, but not here.*
> *There can be no grief,*
> *because, even though I am dead,*
> *I live.*

Affirmation: **We are a small cog in a large wheel, and it must keep turning.**

176
❧

Trance

He fell into a trance,
And saw heaven opened, and a certain vessel
descending unto him, as it had been a great sheet knit
at the four corners, and let down to earth:
Wherein were all manner of four-footed beasts of the
earth, and wild beasts, and creeping things, and fowls
of the air.

THE BIBLE, ACTS OF THE APOSTLES

A TRANCE CAN BE INDUCED by expanding the mind energy, as in meditation, linking up with other dimensions. It enables mediums and healers to have a mind-to-mind contact with those inhabiting these energy levels, so that they can pass on messages or diagnosis to their clients. In my own work as a medium, I was shown how to communicate with my spiritual teachers, which enabled me to practise mediumship and healing. Through meditation I have acquired knowledge that is not available from any other source, and my sole purpose in writing my books has been to pass on that knowledge.

Trance can also be induced through over-indulgence of alcohol and drugs, but the consequences can be death, for unless you have the discipline to return, your mind will leave your body. The shamans who use this method have been indoctrinated from birth, and the elders who watch over them are always alert to any dangers.

The trance state should not be sought by the inexperienced, and – unless you are deeply spiritual and are prepared to live your life by your beliefs – you should avoid it at all costs. The price as an amateur dabbler could be far greater than you are prepared to pay.

Visualisation: You have heard of the trance-like state that people have induced with alcohol and drugs, and you want to experiment. Your mother, aware of the danger, invites you to go shopping with her, but on the way takes the road to the local hospital. With the excuse of visiting a friend she encourages you to enter the psychiatric wing. Your mother asks you to look around. 'I have been helping these young people for some time,' she says. One by one, you are introduced to the most pitiful of human beings. Shocked, you leave the ward. On the way home she tells you that these young people had experimented with alcohol and drugs and had blown their minds. 'Some of them might recover, but there are those whose brains have been damaged beyond repair,' she continues. 'You will never understand the joys of youth until you have lost it, but perhaps this experience will encourage you to resist the temptation to destroy yourself.'

When you are alone again, you know that the future holds no such dangers for you. You have seen the light.

Affirmation: I have the talent or I do not. But I will not seek it through artificial channels.

177

Transfiguration

The change in the appearance of Christ that took place before three disciples (Matthew 17:1–9). The Church festival held in commemoration of this on Aug. 6.

COLLINS ENGLISH DICTIONARY

TRANSFIGURATION IS CAUSED through mind projection, from a spirit who wishes to overshadow the medium's face with that of their own, so that friends and family can look upon them once more, and know that there is life after death. It is a rare phenomenon, and I was honoured to have the opportunity of observing this unbelievable talent performed by a very dedicated medium. Having seen the best, I have been spoiled.

Others have frequently observed transfigurations over my own face, and I have seen the faces of my clients changing into those they had in a past life and I was able to pass on to them details of that life, linking up with problems, likes and dislikes in this one. This knowledge helped cure them of many ills.

Transfiguration is one of those talents that is difficult to believe unless one has seen it. I have seen, and it is one of the many wonders that I will never forget.

Visualisation: **You are looking intensely at the photograph of a woman on the shiny cover of a book. Unable to let go of the image, you are aware that you feel light-headed. Then the face changes and is replaced by that of your own mother, who died several years ago. She smiles, then is gone. You stare hard, trying to bring back the face of someone who was so dear to you but it doesn't work. Disappointed, you look away, and then begin to doubt whether you actually saw her or not. However, the power of her love remains, casting aside those doubts. She returned as she had promised, but in a totally unexpected way.**

Phenomena can rarely be forecast, as it needs many elements to come together at the same time to produce the whole.

Affirmation: Transfiguration exists, and proves beyond doubt that there is life after death.

178

❧

Trouble

*No stranger to trouble myself I am learning to care
for the unhappy.*

VIRGIL
70–19 BC

A TROUBLED MIND will always find trouble, as it is never far away. Shadowing our existence, it hovers, and strikes when we are at our lowest ebb. We must find a way of ignoring it, as we do a naughty child, or it will take over our lives, and the happiness that we all deserve will be relegated to the dark corners of our minds.

When trouble hits you before you have time to take evasive action, then (and only then) do you have to meet it head-on and deal with it. But if you are fearful of what 'might be', then you need to strengthen your resolve and turn it around, saying, 'It may never be.'

Upon receiving clairvoyant diagnosis, I have found that the root cause of many illnesses is worrying about imaginary problems that may never materialise. Only when the mind has been healed have these images disappeared, along with the illness.

There is an old saying, 'Never trouble trouble, 'til trouble troubles you.' I think this should be imprinted on our minds at all times.

Visualisation: Looking at the waves crashing against a harbour wall, you reminisce about the happy times you enjoyed in this small seaport as a child – so different from the life you are living now. Now trouble seems to dog your footsteps. No matter where you go or who you turn to, it is always there, waiting. Someone whispers in your ear, and turning around you are amazed to find a childhood friend standing before you. 'Penny for your thoughts,' he says.

You laugh. 'They're not worth that,' you reply.

Lounging against the wall, you enjoy an easy conversation, and he recalls the image of you as a sunny, smiling child. 'What has happened to you?' he asks.

'Life,' you reply.

He smiles. 'But surely, you of all people know that life is what *you* make it?'

Affirmation: In future, trouble can take a back seat. I want to be happy.

179

❧

Truth

Dare to be true: nothing can need a lie;
A fault, which needs it most, grows two thereby.

GEORGE HERBERT
1593–1633

SOME PEOPLE ARE BORN LIARS, perhaps due to an inherited gene or something they have brought with them from a past life. They are so convincing that, even though you might have known them from childhood, they can make you doubt your own truth if you spend more than five minutes with them. The distress and damage they cause is unimaginable, as the ripples turn into hurricane-like waves that destroy everything in their path. Inevitably, these waves will return to the source and create havoc for the originator, but in the meantime other people's lives are destroyed.

Truth, however, is a different matter. Although it appears at times to be clouded by lies, the truth does have a habit of opening up the book of life and finding the evidence to win the battle. For it *is* a battle – between the seemingly easy way out if you lie, or the harder way if you are honest. In the long run, tell the truth and get it over with. Then you can relax. We all have to take the consequences of our actions, so suffer them and know that, having told the truth, it will not shadow you for the rest of your life. However, if you lie, you must have a good memory and positive proof, for without them you will be exposed for the liar that you are. Stress will be your dubious playmate, and you will never be able to relax.

Visualisation: **Enjoying yourself at a party, you are shocked when you see a friend pocket a small silver object from a display cabinet. You watch in amazement as he nonchalantly walks out of the house. Not wishing to get involved, you dismiss the incident from your mind and carry on partying. The next day you are visited by a detective, and questioned about the incident. You tell the truth. 'Why didn't you stop him?' he asks.**

'I didn't want to get involved,' you reply.

'Well, he certainly tried to involve you,' he remarks, 'He told us that you had stolen it and had asked him to find a buyer.' The detective places a hand on your shoulder. 'You've been lucky this time,' he said, 'because we have the video tape that was set up before the party.' He starts to leave, and then turns back, saying, 'The truth will always out you know, but at least you are on the right track.'

Affirmation: I speak the truth, and seek the truth.

180

Universe

There is a pleasure in the pathless woods,
There is a rapture on the lonely shore,
There is society, where none intrudes,
By the deep sea and music in its roar:
I love not man the less, but Nature more,
From these our interviews, in which I steal
From all I may be, or have been before,
To mingle with the Universe, and feel
What I can ne'er express, yet cannot all conceal.

LORD BYRON
1788–1824

IT IS A MAGICAL FEELING when you know that you will, forever, be a part of the whole. The universe. Whatever it has been, whatever it is, or whatever it will be, we will always belong. The inspirations we receive from the Universal Mind, when used intelligently, are the seeds of creative thought, giving us the ability to see more clearly in this shrouded planet we call Earth.

Your mind is the key to the door of the Universal Mind, because it belongs to that part of the universe. Imprisoned in a heavy physical body, it needs to escape, to remain open to ideas that sustain and aid us through this lifetime. And it is to the universe that our minds return when the physical body ceases to exist.

Through trance and meditation I have seen the beauty of other dimensions that exist in the universe, and those memories will remain with me forever.

What we see through these small portholes that we call eyes is minimal, but with an open mind we can encompass the whole, seen and unseen, which makes for a more spiritual quality of life.

Visualisation: **Trekking through the mountains in India, you are aware of an unseen presence. You can feel it walking by your side, occasionally touching your body. Not wishing to disturb the pleasing effect it has upon you, you stop humming to yourself and walk slowly and silently until you reach a bridge spanning a great gorge. The silence is broken as, hundreds of feet below, you see and hear a river exploding as it seeks out its route among the rocks. Then a voice whispers in your ear, 'Look down and you will see that no matter what obstacles the gorge contains, the river will find its way.' You feel the presence move away and, as it does so, a golden glow lights up the sky as it returns from whence it came. But the memory and the lesson you have learned remain.**

Affirmation: I came from the source, to the source I will return.

181

❧

Unlucky

Therefore, since the world has still
Much good, but much less good than ill,
And while the sun and moon endure
Luck's a chance, but trouble's sure,
I'd face it as a wise man would,
And train for ill and not for good.

A. E. HOUSMAN
1859–1936

ONCE YOU HAVE THE FEELING that you were born unlucky, you have sealed your fate, because you have created a blueprint in your mind that will stay with you forever, unless you can achieve a positive approach to life and cancel it out.

There are families who seem to inherit personalities that generate a negative aura, which flows from one member to another, encouraging unlucky influences. But it doesn't have to be like that. You can and should escape from the negative vibes that cloud a positive outlook. Just tell yourself that you will not entertain the idea that you are unlucky. You make your own luck, and if you think you have had more than your share of bad luck, then you must change it. By doing so, you change the blueprint. Nothing is forever. Changes can and should be made, so that you can get on with living a full and happy life.

Visualisation: You have been trying to get on with your career and your home life, but bad luck seems to follow you around. Tired and exhausted, you visit your mother who listens to your problems. 'Well,' she says, 'our family has always been unlucky, and I suppose we always will be.' Discouraged by her answer, you suddenly realise that the negativity handed down from generation to generation had actually attracted the bad luck. Like an illness it was infectious, and all the family were of the opinion that it was also incurable.

Determined to find the way out of this kind of reasoning, you begin to stimulate the positive side of your nature. Your boss is impressed, your partner is impressed, and your career takes off. On visiting your mother again you tell her of your luck, 'I'm pleased for you,' she says, 'but I can't understand why you should be so lucky in such an unlucky family. The gods must be looking after you.'

You smile, and say, 'Maybe. But I am also looking after myself.'

Affirmation: There is a way out, but there have to be changes in my mental attitude to life.

182

❧

Unreasonable

The reasonable man adapts himself to the world: the unreasonable one persists in trying to adapt the world to himself. Therefore all progress depends on the unreasonable man.

GEORGE BERNARD SHAW
1856–1950

THERE CAN BE NO EXCUSE for persistent unreasonable behaviour. It is disruptive and adds unnecessary stress to already difficult situations. There are no winners in a situation like this, only losers. Experience of these personalities tells us that the unreasonable person is eventually cold-shouldered by friends and family, and their victims may suffer reduced circumstances through ill health.

There are countless excuses for occasional unreasonable behaviour, and in retrospect most of us would not have behaved in this fashion unless we had been pushed by other unreasonable people. Unfortunately, it brings us down to their level, so it is far better to keep our self-respect and to resist the temptation to mirror their words and actions.

Visualisation: You have been keeping company with your new boyfriend for six months. When you first met him, you were stylish, always ready to have fun, and had many friends. Unfortunately, from the moment you met, he criticised everything about you. Because you loved him, you changed everything about yourself, and have cut yourself off from your friends.

Meeting a friend one day in a dress shop, you realise how much you have changed when she doesn't recognise you. Turning you around, she makes you look into a long mirror, saying, 'Look at yourself.' You are shocked at the image before you – no make-up, drab clothes, old shoes, no jewellery. But worst of all is the haunted look in your eyes.

On the way home you call at the hairdressers and have a hairdo, a make-up session and manicure. When you get home you put on your short skirt, high heels and jewellery, and you make a few calls to friends, arranging to meet them that evening in one of your old haunts.

Your boyfriend calls, and when he is faced with the old you, you argue. The futility of the situation becomes clear when he accuses you of unreasonable behaviour, and you ask him to leave. When he has gone, you look into the mirror; your eyes are shining and alive once more, you know that in future you will live life your own way, and send all unreasonable people back to the negative world they inhabit.

Affirmation: Persistent unreasonable behaviour is inexcusable.

183

❧

Vibrations

Lift not the painted veil which those who live
Call Life.

PERCY BYSSHE SHELLEY
1792–1822

THE EVER-CHANGING, rotating universe is dependent on energy waves that create slipstreams, vortices, rivers and seas, most of them unseen. But the vibrational force never stops, and encompasses everything that exists.

We can feel the vibrations emanating from person to person, and these give a guide as to whether we want to be near someone or not, as negative energy vibes give out an unpleasant sensation. It is possible sometimes to feel the waves of telepathy when someone is thinking about us.

Inanimate objects vibrate with the mind energies that have been absorbed by their owners, and those gifted with psychic talents can 'read' them.

The best way to live our lives is to go with the flow, energising and stimulating our bodies and minds so that we can become part of the whole. If we are lucky, the universe will let us glimpse the wonders that exist in other dimensions.

Visualisation: **You have been invited to a party, and although you are not a party person the invitation is from the Chairman of your company, so you feel you should attend. As you dress for the evening you suddenly feel vital and positive, as though you had taken some kind of stimulant. You remember that you had felt like this before when something important was about to happen.**

Later, whilst you are mingling with other guests, you feel a force boring its way into your back. You turn, and across the room make eye contact with the only person in the world you would want to share your life with, someone you have been trying to trace for a very long time.

Affirmation: I can feel the vibrations that sustain me.

184

❦

Vocabulary

Many terms which have now dropped out of favour,
will be revived, and those that are at present
respectable will drop out, if usage so choose, with
whom resides the decision and the judgement and
the code of speech.

HORACE
65 – 8 BC

THERE IS NOTHING quite so frustrating as trying to express yourself when you can't find the right phrase or word to do it. The dictionary is the greatest book in the world – every word is meaningful and expressive, and we should become acquainted with as many of them as possible if we are to make any impression at all. So many people have such a small vocabulary that they are destined to spend the rest of their lives in the company of others who are as limited as they are.

You may have a special talent, but without the ability to communicate you will have to ask someone to mediate for you when discussing opportunities. This works quite well until they become unavailable, when you will feel humiliated and inferior. Do not let this happen.

Carry a small dictionary around with you. When you feel that you can remember and understand a number of words, buy a small grammar book, and use those words to make sentences that you can apply to your life.

Words are magical. It is never too late to find a way of bringing the magic into your vocabulary.

Visualisation: You have been invited to demonstrate, before a group of businessmen, an invention that you have been working on for five years. Your hopes are high as you proceed to show them what it can do. Impressed, they ask you to lunch in the Chairman's office. One by one they try to engage you in conversation, but you are tongue-tied because you cannot express yourself very well unless you are talking about your work. Although your invention has impressed them enough to offer you a contract, you do not forget the humiliating experience. In the autumn you attend evening classes for English language.

Affirmation: My vocabulary can always be improved.

185

Voice

Her voice was ever soft,
Gentle and low, an excellent thing in a woman.

WILLIAM SHAKESPEARE
1564–1616

LISTENING TO A BEAUTIFUL VOICE is a divine experience. I have listened to many beautiful voices, many of them recorded. Some have touched my soul and will be with me forever, while others were a fleeting but nonetheless memorable experience. The impression they all leave behind is the choice we have to make our voice into a thing of beauty, or to neglect it and make it ugly.

There is so much that can be done to enhance the voice that I am constantly amazed when I am bombarded by repellent singing and speech on television, radio or in public. There is no excuse for it, only laziness and arrogance.

When I encourage young people to improve their speech, they remark that their family and friends will laugh at them. They are missing the point. There are all kinds of people in the world, and each of us needs to be able to communicate with every one of them. Life is about change. The voice is the key that will open many doors that would otherwise be closed – it has to be clear, concise and understandable, or we will be ignored. Control over our voices, like our lives, is ours; we have the choice for what is right for us.

If you would like to improve your voice, then record your voice on tape, and listen. Keep practising until you are satisfied that you have done everything possible to make this instrument, your voice, give out the best tones that you are capable of without losing the character that sustains it.

Visualisation: **Alone on the top of a mountain, you are captivated by the most beautiful singing you have ever heard. Then you hear voices speaking nearby, eloquent and mesmerising. You want to hear more of these wonderful tones, but feel as though someone is drawing you back, away from this incredible experience. Then you wake – it was a dream. But the beauty of those voices is unforgettable, and you seek help to improve the part of you that you have, so far, ignored.**

Affirmation: I shall make my voice a thing of beauty.

186
❦

Vulgarity

No terms of moderation takes place with the vulgar.

FRANCIS BACON
1561–1626

THERE ARE SO MANY vulgar acts committed these days that many children believe it is normal and natural to behave in this way. Innocent children are bombarded by vulgarity on television and, unless parents are vigilant, it can have drastic effects on their behaviour because they don't know how to deal with the images and words they absorb. They repeat the phrases they hear, even though they have no idea what they mean – if it is said on television, then as far as they're concerned it's acceptable. Their minds are being messed up with so much violence and vulgarity that we cannot blame them for growing up into lager louts.

Obscene and vulgar words are hurled at anyone who will not give way to threats, and people live in fear of abuse. Even on the roads drivers make vulgar signs to each other. How base can you get? And yet this behaviour is accepted as the norm. Unless laws can be passed to fine vulgar and obscene acts on the spot, this problem will not go away, but will only get worse.

Visualisation: **Driving down a country lane with your young family, another car pulls in to allow you to pass and you raise your hand to acknowledge the courtesy. Your young son questions the act, and you explain that you are thanking that person as he had made it easier for you to continue your journey. Then, a car pulls up behind you and hoots non-stop. Not wishing to encourage any unpleasantness, you find a lay-by so that you can let them overtake. As they do so, the driver of the other vehicle makes a vulgar and obscene gesture. Your son asks you what it means, and you tell him that the driver was being very rude, because he was unable to communicate in any other way. 'That's why I encourage you to read, rather than look at television,' you tell him. 'It enables you to communicate intelligently.'**

Affirmation: If I have to endure vulgarity, I will not stoop to the same level.

187

❧

Walking

Who is the third who walks always beside you?
When I count, there are only you and I together
But when I look ahead up the white road
There is always another one walking beside you.

T. S. ELIOT
1888–1965

WALKING IS THE ONE THING that, if fit, we can all do. Every day, without fail, we should walk until tired, then turn around and walk back, breathing deeper and feeling our lungs working overtime.

Sounds exhausting? That's because you are out of practice, but don't worry, you have the rest of your life to catch up. As long as you walk more than you did last year, you'll be doing well.

Because of the danger of being accosted, women do have problems walking in deserted areas, even with their dogs, so try to walk with a friend, or exercise somewhere you know you will not be alone. It is appalling that women should be at risk in beautiful, natural areas, because sometimes they need to be alone, away from the children, the housework, the telephone and the hundred and one jobs they have to deal with. If you live alone or where it is impossible to walk in safety, buy a treadmill or similar machine from a reputable dealer. That way you will be able to exercise in peace. Keeping the windows open whilst exercising is an added benefit.

We could all add a few more steps to our daily routine, so get on with it – no excuses!

Visualisation: It is winter, and the countryside has a light covering of snow. Your friend calls by and urges you to take a walk with her over the fields with her dogs. You make the excuse that you are feeling tired, that you had a late night, that you ache all over, but she will not listen. Finding your coat, she laughingly forces you to put it on and pushes you out of the door. Moaning and groaning, you start walking beside her whilst she throws sticks for her animals to retrieve. Suddenly you find that you are breathing more easily than you have done for weeks, that your sinuses are clear, and as you walk up the hill you feel your lungs expanding. Your body is glowing, and you can't remember a time when you felt so vital. Telling your friend about it, she laughs. 'Of course you feel good,' she declares. 'You're getting oxygen into your lungs instead of breathing in the dust-laden atmosphere of your centrally heated flat. If you had stayed indoors much longer your immune system would have given up the ghost.'

Affirmation: I am determined to walk a little further each day.

188

Warfare

There never was a good war, or a bad peace.

BENJAMIN FRANKLIN
1706–1790

WHEN WILL WE EVER LEARN? Every day we are bombarded by stories and pictures from around the world, showing human beings blowing each other to bits. There has been no progress, and some people have sunk to such depths that they are immune to the suffering of others. It seems to get worse, not better, and whilst people are suffering, others are sitting around tables talking about peace and how to achieve it. Should they interfere or not? Whilst they deliberate in comfort, the fate of those poor stricken people around the world who have no one to turn to, no one to speak up for them, hangs in the balance. I am not a physical campaigner, but I believe that many people feel as I do. In this paragraph I am using the only weapon I have, the ability to put my feelings into words, hoping that it will be read by someone, somewhere, with the courage, determination and authority to do something about it. We need a world force, one that can go into any country at any time, to stop warfare before it starts. I believe that this can be done. Red tape the world over consumes time and wastes the billions of pounds which could be used to rebuild Third World countries. Instead we indulge in peace talks that take years, while the killing goes on.

I know that good work *is* being done, most of it by the compassionate people in the field who are prepared to give their lives to help their fellow men. They are the heroes, the ones who should have the medals, but like all minority groups they are often overlooked when it is time to hand out the honours.

Warfare also destroys the environment we live in. We are all responsible if we do not shout about it in whatever way we can. Writing a letter to those who could do something about it would be a start.

I am not going to give a visualisation for this piece because it speaks for itself, but we will not be able to hold our heads high until the suffering stops.

Affirmation: I will think about it, and then act.

189

✤

Water divining

Lovely are the curves of the white owl sweeping
Wavy in the dusk lit by one large star.
Lone on the fir-branch, his rattle-note unvaried,
Brooding o'er the gloom, spins the brown eve-jar.
Darker grows the valley, more and more forgetting:
So were it with me if forgetting could be willed.
Tell the grassy-hollow that holds the bubbling well-spring,
Tell it to forget the source that keeps it filled.

GEORGE MEREDITH
1828–1909

WATER DIVINERS ARE INVALUABLE, especially in areas where every drop of water is worth more than its weight in gold. Most experts have learnt their skill by dowsing, which embraces many things. For instance, some famous healers use dowsing as a means of obtaining a diagnosis; other diviners can seek out minerals, gold, iron, gas, and more. However, water diviners are special, because most of their work involves helping the individual and not themselves: finding a source of water for a small farmer so that he can sink a well and water his cattle when there is a drought, or divining a source of water for people who live in isolated desert conditions, and who otherwise have to walk miles for their water, bringing life and sustenance where there had been none. All of these things make water divining worthwhile.

Visualisation: You are walking over fields with a water diviner, whom you have asked to show you the first steps in divining. Handing you a couple of forked twigs, he says, 'I cut these from the witch hazel myself.' He shows you how to hold the twigs in front of you, and tells you to start walking in a straight line. 'When you feel the twigs pulling down, then you have found something. Could be water, could be anything.' He makes you walk and walk, sometimes in circles, but always at his direction. All the time he watches the twigs you are holding, and occasionally he puts a coloured sticker in the ground. When you are thoroughly worn out, he suggests you put away the twigs and walk with him to the stickers. 'I have put these on the ground as they indicate whether you detected anything.'

'Well, did I?' you ask excitedly.

He smiles, and says, 'Yes – dead bodies and water!' He explains that the hazel twigs that you held were drawn towards the spots where he had buried some dead pheasants and an underwater stream, both of which elicited more force than other items he had also placed underground. 'You can either train as a water diviner or use your talent to find dead bodies,' he says. When you remark that there wouldn't be much use for a dowser who finds bodies, he regales you with the stories of dowsers who have worked with the police all over the world.

Affirmation: Dowsing can be my eyes, to open up hitherto unseen and unknown mysteries.

190

❦

Weak-willed

Oh, Vanity of vanities!
How wayward the decrees of Fate are;
How very weak the very wise,
How very small the very great are!

WILLIAM MAKEPEACE THACKERAY
1811–1863

BEING WEAK-WILLED can lead people into circumstances that could destroy them. Very few admit to this fault in their character, because it needs positive effort to combat it, and laziness is inherent in the weak-willed. The biggest problem is that they find it easier, and sometimes more exciting, to say *yes* than *no*. It is amazing how resilient these people are; they go through hell, fire and water to carry out the wishes of others. Their desire to please cancels out the laziness. Therein lies the cure, but only if they can find a trustworthy and loving friend or partner who will be prepared to spend time helping them. In these circumstances, the weak part of their nature would be only too willing to be dominated, but at least their agreement would lead to a more meaningful existence.

Visualisation: As a father, you are concerned when your son shows signs of being weak-willed. You know all the pitfalls because you had been weak-willed in your youth, and through that fault in your character, nearly lost your life, so you decide to take him out for the day. Walking beside a river, you stop at a point where the water is rushing over a weir. 'I was once stupid enough to listen to friends of mine and throw myself into that whirlpool at the bottom,' you remark. Your son questions you about the incident, and you tell him that because of your then weak nature, you allowed them to get you drunk, and then obeyed their orders. Taking a deep breath, you say, 'That was the day I nearly lost my life.' You go on to tell him about other idiotic pranks you got into because you couldn't say no. When you have finished, your son looks sad. 'It sounds dreadful. What made you change?' he asks.

'I was lucky enough to meet your mother when I was still young,' you tell him. 'She was the nicest person I had ever known, and I loved her and wanted to look after her. She had faith in me and I couldn't let her down.' You pause. 'Sometimes, though, I am totally humiliated by the memories of the things I did in those early days. I wouldn't want you to suffer the same fate.'

Your son's behaviour changes during the next few months, and you know it is his love for you that has given him strength.

Affirmation: I will say no to idiotic suggestions, and choose my own positive path.

191
❧

Wealth

Let not ambition mock their useful toil,
Their homely joys, and destiny obscure;
Nor grandeur hear with a disdainful smile,
The short and simple annals of the poor.

THOMAS GRAY
1.716–1771

I WOULD PLACE HEALTH, happiness and wealth in that order. If you are healthy, you can work toward becoming wealthy. If you are happy and healthy, then your task would be more pleasurable. But wealth, although it can give one the creature comforts, has very little going for it if the stress of managing it makes you miserable and ill.

Inherited wealth can be a nightmare if you haven't the strength of character to side-step the many minefields that await you. Having a weak-willed heir who likes the good life can have far-reaching and disastrous consequences.

Being financially independent brings many problems. You never know who your friends are, or who you can trust. There are hundreds of professional hangers-on waiting to pounce, some of them extremely attractive until you get to know them properly, and when you do, it is probably too late. Wealth *can* open doors, but you may not like what is behind them.

I am sure that there are very wealthy people who have friends they can trust, but they are probably wealthy too, as wealth isolates the rich from the poor. It has always been this way and always will be until spirituality touches each and every one. We may have to wait a long time for that.

Visualisation: **You have been invited to join a house party at a magnificent country house. Unfortunately no one seems to be happy, concerned as they are about their stocks and shares, their businesses, the upkeep of their expensive homes. In fact, they all look and sound thoroughly miserable.**

When you arrive back home, you feel the happy vibrations before you open the door. Walking into your small, comfortable rooms, you thank God for the gifts of laughter and fun that have always been your constant companions. Thinking about the weekend, you realise that wealth, in the wrong hands, creates a wall of suspicion and negativity, encapsulating those who own it in a vacuum of loneliness and despair.

Affirmation: My health and happiness are more important than wealth.

192

❦

Witches

*And they think we're burning witches when we're only
burning weeds.*

G. K. CHESTERTON
1874–1936

THE WORD 'WITCHES' brings a tingle to those who love magic, mystery and the danger of the unknown. It is the stuff of fables – unfortunately, I have to include some facts!

White witches were the first mediums and healers, and they practised the art of healing hundreds of years before modern medicine. They lived isolated lives from choice, because being close to nature enables the psychic gift to blossom and mature. Their talents also encompassed herbal medicine because the ingredients were readily available, and people knew more about the earth and its secrets than we do today.

So why were they burnt at the stake? Their good deeds were common knowledge in their small communities, but church leaders feared they were losing control, and wanted to hang on to their own power. Because they were not gifted in healing like the white witches, they destroyed those who were. Unfortunately, they knew nothing of Universal Law, the ultimate judge of good and bad.

Witches are no longer burnt at the stake, but fear of these incredible gifts still attracts negative comments. Remember this: Those who fear the most, have the most to fear.

Visualisation: **You are taken back hundreds of years to a place in the woods where a white witch lives. Dressed in a long black skirt, shawl and round black hat, she comes out to greet you. Inside her small but comfortable wooden home, she spreads out dried herbs and places some of them, along with other roots and leaves, into a pot. 'I am brewing a cure for aches and pains in the body,' she explains. Then her black cat walks into the room and brushes against her legs, surveying you with a watchful eye.**

Think about what you have just read. There is nothing unusual about any of it. People wore black in those days because it was practical. They had few clothes, sometimes only one change, and the shawl and hat were to keep her warm. The dried herbs around the house were exactly the same as some of the species we keep in our gardens and homes today.

The black cat? Cats sense unpleasant vibes before we do, and simply would not associate with anyone evil. It is all perfectly normal stuff that has been blown out of proportion and has been kept alive by those who love dressing up.

Affirmation: White witches are healers. Nothing has changed.

193

❦

Work

*Perfect freedom is reserved for the man who lives by
his own work, and in that work does what he wants to do.*

R. G. COLLINGWOOD
1889–1943

WORK HAS OFTEN BEEN the saviour for many who have suffered terrible losses and tragedy. The ability to shut out the rest of the world and concentrate in a positive and creative way takes away the impact of the two-edged sword on which, without work, we might impale ourselves.

Work, and the financial support it brings, keeps stress at bay. It is necessary to our health and happiness, and does not deserve the abuse that is often directed toward it. If you hate the work that you do but cannot change it for financial reasons, then find something that you love to do for a hobby. If you can eventually make money from it, so much the better.

The need to work is sometimes only recognised when work is no longer available. Those who retire become bored if they have nothing to do. There are only so many holidays to take, so many friends and relatives to visit – the rest is up to them. Women of retirement age tend to carry on doing the same things they have always done – working like mad to keep the home and family together.

Visualisation: **You have been made redundant, and are unable to find similar employment that will enable you to keep you and your family in the manner to which you have become accustomed. The positive attitude of your family and friends supports your determination to win through, but all the avenues turn out to be dead ends. To keep your head above water, you try anything. Whilst working at the cash desk at the local all-night garage, you engage in conversation with a customer. You mention your real career, and he takes out a card and says, 'Give me a ring.' When you look at the card, you find that he is in the same business as you used to be. Later that month, after you have been interviewed and have met other members of the firm, he offers you a top job.**

Never say never, and never turn down an opportunity, no matter how small, because it could lead you down unexpected and lucrative paths.

Affirmation: Work is food for the soul.

194

❧

World

You daren't handle high explosives; but you're all ready
to handle honesty and truth and justice and the whole
duty of man, and kill one another at that game. What
a country! What a world!

GEORGE BERNARD SHAW
1856–1950

THE BEAUTIES OF THIS PLANET are usually overshadowed by the stories of the persecution of its inhabitants around the world. Innocents suffer for the sake of the egomaniacs who have, through terror and torture, become rulers of their particular kingdoms. The pity of it is that we are all so insignificant in the scheme of things, and in the final analysis Universal Law will be the judge. There can be no excuse for the perpetrators of these crimes. They are crimes against the individual, against humanity and against God, and everyone who loves this planet that is our home should protect it and its inhabitants to the best of their ability – even if this is only to put pen to paper, demanding that everyone has the right to live and enjoy the wonders of the world. We should not strive for riches, but for the chance to live out our lives in peace.

Visualisation: You are living in a world where peace reigns in every kingdom in the world. The environment is healthy, and the people are happy and industrious. Every town, every village, has rebelled against the sordid side of human nature and has embraced spiritual thought. There are no dictators, no rulers, but each person takes responsibility for their own deeds. Is it a dream? Perhaps. But it is a dream that we should all be seeking, all the time, within our own environment. Spirituality has to be at the forefront of all our thinking if our children are not to be lost in the maze of materialism that causes the mind-bending terrors the world is now experiencing.

Affirmation: I will, to the best of my ability, help the world to help itself.

195

❧

Writing

Abou Ben Adhem (may his tribe increase!)
Awoke one night from a deep dream of peace,
And saw, within the moonlight in his room,
Making it rich, and like a lily in bloom,
An angel writing in a book of gold:-
Exceeding peace had made Ben Adhem bold,
And to the presence in the room he said,
'What writest thou?' – The vision raised its head,
And with a look made of all sweet accord,
Answered, 'The names of those who love the Lord.'

LEIGH HUNT
1784–1859

As a writer, I cannot think of anything more satisfying than to be able to put thoughts into words, knowing that we acquire knowledge through the same process. Thinking expands the mind energy and enables it to link into our particular source of inspiration.

Books are worlds within worlds, containing imagery and knowledge that can open up hitherto unknown avenues for the reader. The wonders of these worlds have been painstakingly written down, incorporating the talent and imagination of the writer. Without them, ignorance would reign. Writing is also therapeutic, and can cure many ills.

Visualisation: You have a deep and apparently incurable hatred for someone who has treated you badly. It seems that nothing can ease the pain caused by the emotional scars you have been carrying for so long. Then, one day, you pick up a pen and paper to record your thoughts. As the words tumble out of your mind on to the paper, you can feel all the pent-up emotions leaving. Your head feels lighter, and the ache in your heart disappears. With renewed effort, you continue over the next two weeks to shower the paper with the thoughts that have been imprisoned for so long in the dark corners of your mind. When you are finally sick to death of the memories, you know that you are cured, and that for the rest of your life you can use this method as an escape route.

Affirmation: I will write down all negative thoughts, and never again retain them in the dark corners of my mind.

196

❧

Xenoglossia

The unexamined life is not worth living.

469–399 BC

XENOGLOSSIA IS THE ABILITY claimed by some mediums to speak a language with which they are unfamiliar. To the uninitiated it sounds rather far-fetched, but at the beginning of my own mediumship I was often amazed to hear spirit voices speaking in strange tongues. Through sheer boredom, however, I stopped listening. I could see no point whatsoever in wasting time on something I didn't understand when I could be passing on loving and meaningful messages to my sitters. Later, I learned that this is a very common occurrence when one is going through the first stages of mediumship, and not wishing to appear stupid, novices sometimes make the excuse that the messages are from another planet!

Visualisation: You are receiving messages from a medium when she suddenly begins to speak gibberish. Not wishing to be rude you listen for five minutes then interrupt her, saying, 'I'm sorry, but I can't understand you.' Furious at the interruption, she tells you that it is your loss as she was giving you information from another planet. As you are about to leave, you turn to her and say, 'Maybe next time you could give me a translation?'

Affirmation: If I cannot understand the message, it is of no use.

197

❦

Yarns

*I must go down to the sea again, to the vagrant
gypsy life,
To the gull's way and the whale's way where the
wind's like a whetted knife;
And all I ask is a merry yarn from a laughing
fellow-rover,
And quiet sleep and a sweet dream when the long
trick's over.*

JOHN MASEFIELD
1878–1967

WHEN I LISTEN TO YARNS I am always amazed at the inventiveness of the story-teller. Their imagination knows no bounds, as adults and children alike sit spellbound as the stories unfold. What a gift! The world would be a sorrier place if we didn't have the laughter, the leg-pulling, and indeed the miserable cynics who themselves are the butt of laughter when they disbelieve the yarns. We need these people. So if you have the gift of the story-teller, enhance it, and brighten up all of our lives.

Visualisation: Enjoying a drink in your favourite pub, you notice that people are crowding around a man at the bar. Not wishing to miss out, you join them. The man is telling yarns about his sea-fishing expeditions, and the tales he tells are so amazing that you stand rooted to the spot for almost an hour. The more he drinks the more imaginative he becomes. When he eventually staggers out of the pub you learn that he has never been to sea in his life.

'Why do you listen and buy him drinks?' you ask.

'Because he is the greatest yarn teller in the business,' one man replies, 'and he brightens up our lives with his fantasies.'

Affirmation: There is always a bit of wisdom in a yarn. Look for it.

198

❧

Yearning

Give me your tired, your poor,
Your huddled masses yearning to breathe free.

EMMA LAZARUS
1849–1887

WE ALL HAVE STRONG emotional longings at some time in our lives, but when the hunger never ceases despite there being very little hope of the dream materialising, it is time to move on to the next stage in your life. Yearning can be a simple hankering, or a terrible craving, therefore it must be controlled before it gets out of hand. There is a life waiting for you; find it and get rid of the yearning that is threatening to ruin your future.

Visualisation: **For two years you have been longing to meet someone with whom you can share your life. The dream never fades, but realising that it may never happen you decide to give yourself a break, and take a long sea voyage. Two months later you have met the person with whom you can share your dreams. Without that first positive step you could still be waiting.**

Affirmation: I will turn the yearning into a learning experience.

199

❧

Yoga

Dark-heaving – boundless, endless, and sublime,
The image of eternity.

LORD BYRON
1788–1824

YOGA IS A HINDU SYSTEM of philosophic meditation designed to effect a reunion with the Universal Spirit, bringing physical, mental, moral, and spiritual growth. Beginning with easy exercises it improves health and, in the more advanced stages, provides mental well-being that balances the physical with its energy counterpart. The word *Yoga* is derived from the Sanskrit root 'YUJ', which means 'join'. There are many divisions but the aim is the same. The most common practice is that of Hatha Yoga, which gives one a sense of physical well-being, and is a preparation for the more advanced techniques.

If you would like to learn how to breathe and exercise correctly then buy one of the many yoga books or, preferably join a yoga class. But do make sure that you choose a teacher that has graduated through the Wheel of Yoga, or someone that has been approved by some other yoga organisation.

I will give you a simple visualisation exercise to introduce you to the peaceful and spiritual world of yoga.

Visualisation: **Standing at an open window, you breathe deeply. When you feel relaxed lie down on a soft pad on the floor. Put your hands under your knees – you can join hands if you wish – then start rocking back and forth, keeping your spine rounded. Have fun with this exercise. You may like to straighten your legs as you swing backwards and then bend them again as you swing forwards but keep moving.**

When you have finished visualising this exercise try it for real when you find the time. It really works wonders. ·

Affirmation: Yoga cannot be practised in a haphazard way. I will listen and learn.

200

Youth

How beautiful is youth, that is always slipping away!
Whoever wants to be happy, let him be so: about
tomorrow there's no knowing.

LORENZO DE' MEDICI
1449–1492

THE ELDERLY TALK CONSTANTLY about their youth. With bright eyes and a happy smile, they recall incidents they know could never be repeated. And yet, the young are disdainful of the few years they have been around. It is strange, for whilst their elders long for their lost youth, the young are longing to add the years to their life-span, demonstrating that human beings are never (and will never be) satisfied with the way things are.

If you are young, do as many things as you can, and seek as much knowledge as you can, because later in life you will find great happiness recalling the memory of what you were.

Visualisation: You meet with old friends and reminisce about the escapades of your youth. Laughing and joking with each other, it becomes apparent to you all that without these experiences you would not be sitting, as you are now, reliving them and sharing the same rapport. You are also aware that physical appearance matters very little when the mind is ageless.

Affirmation: The mind, forever young, will overcome the ageing experience.

201

❧

Zest

I love all that thou lovest,
Spirit of Delight:
The fresh Earth in new leaves dressed,
And the starry night;
Autumn evening, and the morn
When the golden mists are born.

PERCY BYSSHE SHELLEY
1792–1822

I HOPE THIS BOOK will give you the zest to live your life to the full. *Zest*. What a wonderful word! Invigorating, exciting, and full of joy. If you spend the rest of your life working towards this goal you will have fun. It may be that you have already felt the full impact of this feeling, or that someone else has brought it into your life. If you have, hold that dream and never let it go, for one day it will return, perhaps when you least expect it.

Visualisation: It is winter, and you are on a skiing holiday. As you are experienced you decide to take the ski lift to the top of one of the highest mountains. As the lift carries you over the snow-covered landscape to the summit, you feel the adrenaline kick in. Before you begin your downward journey you can feel that zest for life that you always feel when you are at the point of no return, and which has always given you the courage to fulfil your dreams.

Affirmation: I will look for the zest in life and make my dreams come true.

INDEX

If you wish to receive distant healing, books, tapes or teaching brochures, please write to the address below:

Betty Shine
P.O. Box 1009
Hassocks
West Sussex
BN6 8XS

Please enclose a stamped and addressed envelope for a reply. Thank you.

POSTSCRIPT

When *A Mind of Your Own* was first published, it became obviously very quickly from the huge amount of mail I received daily that people hated to leave behind the comfort and advice in this book when they left home. As a result, two pocket books have been compiled, *Clear Your Mind* and *Free Your Mind*, each containing 75 extracts from the parent book. Filled with quotations, insights and affirmations, these little books of life have become very popular in their own right and you might wish to seek them out at your local bookseller.

CLEAR YOUR MIND   0-00-653098-2
FREE YOUR MIND   0-00-653183-0